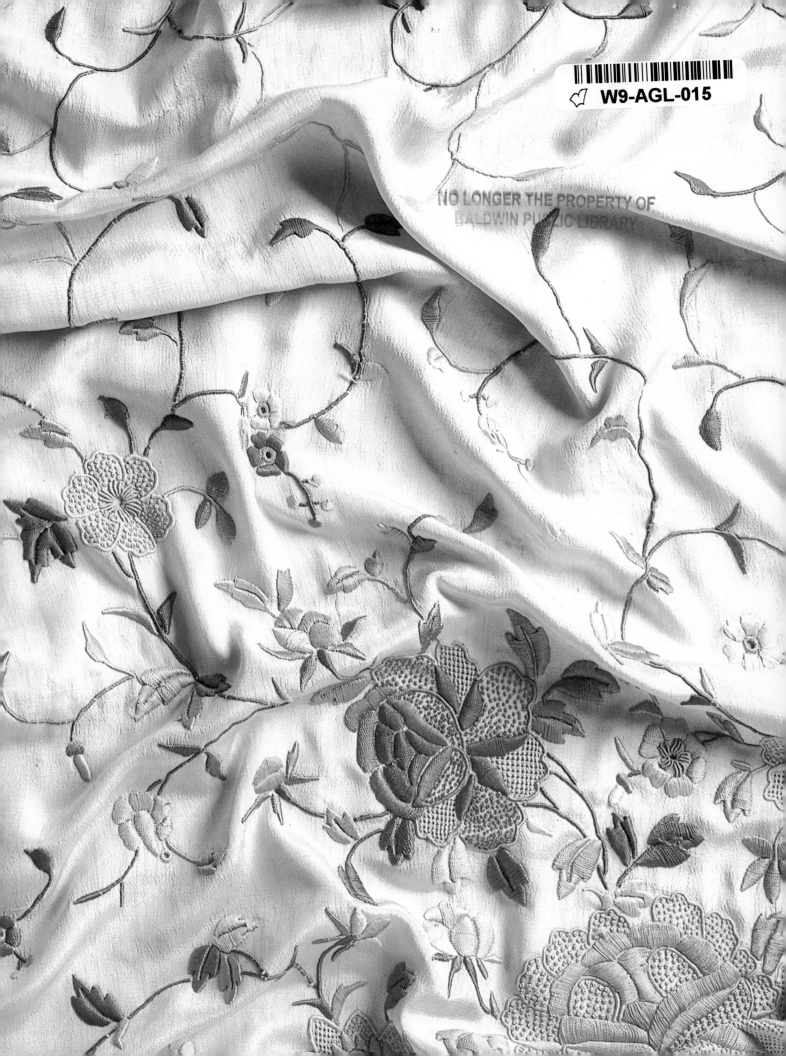

VICTORIAN CRAFTS

VICTORIAN CRAFTS

Over forty charming projects to make from the Victorian era

Edited by **Tracy Marsh**

T

Trafalgar Square Publishing
NORTH POMFRET, VERMONT

First published in the United States of America in 1993
by Trafalgar Square Publishing, North Pomfret, Vermont 05053

Copyright © 1992 Tracy Marsh Publications Pty Ltd and Weldon Russell Pty Ltd

Editorial Co-ordination: Debi McCulloch, Dawn Titmus
Photography: Adam Bruzzone
Photography Stylist: Tony Balzan
Copy Editor: Liz Burpee
Designer: Kathie Baxter Smith
Production: Jane Hazell, Dianne Leddy

Library of Congress Catalog Card Number: 93–60143

ISBN: 0 943955 75 0

Produced by Tracy Marsh Publications Pty Ltd
Ground Floor, 97 Rose Street, Chippendale NSW 2008, Australia, in association with
Weldon Russell Pty Ltd, 107 Union Street, North Sydney NSW 2060, Australia.

Typeset by Jackie Hannan, TMP
Printed in Singapore by Kyodo Printing Co. Ltd

⎯ Notes to Readers ⎯

BEFORE YOU BEGIN

Many of the projects in *Victorian Crafts* refer to the same embroidery stitches, materials and techniques. The stitches used are listed at the beginning of each project and it is recommended that you refer to the Stitch Glossary on pages 158–164 and practice the techniques before working your project. Before you begin, read through all the instructions carefully and acquaint yourself with unfamiliar techniques and materials by referring to the Glossary on pages 165–167.

TERMINOLOGY

batting = wadding
calico = cotton fabric with small prints, often floral (sprig muslin)
embroidery floss = embroidery thread
muslin = calico
rabbet = rebate
wooden clothes pins = dolly pegs

All other materials used in the projects are given in American terminology, with British, Australian or New Zealand equivalents in parentheses where needed. Also see the Glossary.

USING THE PATTERNS

Some of the patterns have been reduced to fit the pages conveniently. They have been drawn on a squared grid. To enlarge the patterns to full size, purchase or draw a grid with squares 1 x 1 in. (2.5 x 2.5 cm) allowing the same amount of squares as indicated in the scaled patterns.

Using a sharp pencil, begin drawing at a point where the pattern line coincides with the intersection of four squares. Mark a dot at this point.

Repeat this process, marking dots at each point where the pattern line intersects with a line of the grid. Carefully join up the dots with smooth, even lines, then transfer all the labels and markings to each pattern piece. Cut out each pattern piece ready to use.

Contents

Introduction

WHEN Victoria was crowned Queen of England in 1837, Britain and America were experiencing massive industrial developments and changing lifestyles. Throughout the century industrial and scientific advances engendered an immense increase in national wealth and a yearning from the people for quality of life and culture. The Victorian era, as it became known (Victoria lived until 1901), was a time of improved standards of decency and morality, and an unquestioning acceptance of authority.

Victorian homes of the wealthy classes were always filled to the brim with favorite objects that allowed for personal expression of style. The colors and patterns of the Victorian era were quite distinctive—floral patterns were prominent and often in strong, rich colors as well as pastels. The Victorians were very fond of nature, and this was reflected indoors in the floral crafts that adorned everything—quilts, embroidered cushions, carpets, dried flowers, and potpourri. The nineteenth century was distinctly different from other periods in its great stylistic elegance and a return to romanticism and sentimentality.

The increase in wealth meant that large numbers of middle-class women were now able to hire servants, thus acquiring more leisure time for themselves. Victorian women loved to do "fancy work", a term that covered a multitude of different techniques, including tapestry, cross stitch, heirloom sewing, lace work, découpage, and bead work. They would spend many hours in their parlors stitching and pasting to produce exquisite handmade crafts and needlework either to adorn their homes or to share as gifts.

Opposite: One can stop and reflect on the elegance of the Victorian era.
Above: Gathered mementos of the past.

CHAPTER 1

Child's Play

THE INNOCENCE of childhood was never stronger than in the Victorian era. Victorian children were the center of the family unit—they were doted upon and were given toys and games galore. Little girls played with porcelain dolls, stuffed animals and miniature dolls' houses; little boys played with soldiers and pull toys.

Children were given lavish birthday parties that included Punch-and-Judy shows, hurdy-gurdies and elaborate fancy-dress costumes. However, Victorian children were also taught never to be careless or wasteful with their toys, because it was felt that this attitude could influence their characters forever. They were also encouraged to make gifts for others in order to learn the value of giving.

Above: The Pop-up Jester is a child's delight.
Opposite: The miniature Victorian Doll's House will become a
treasured family heirloom.

Miniature Victorian Doll's House

It was during the Victorian era that the doll's house truly came into its own as a child's toy that was designed to be played with. Yet you can create an heirloom for your family to cherish by making your own doll's house. A first doll's house can be based on a relatively simple design that is well within the reaches of the hobby woodworker. The Miniature Victorian Doll's House is made from custom board that offers ease of construction and maximum strength. It could also be made from exterior-quality plywood, if this is more easily obtainable.

Study the construction diagram thoroughly before starting. If you can visualize the various steps of the project, you will anticipate problems and have time to sort them out. The house is made in two distinct sections—the rooms and the roof, which lifts off. This design feature allows a transformer to be located in the roof cavity at a later stage, in case you decide to add lights. It also allows the house to be moved without damage to the vulnerable angles of the roof.

This doll's house is painted in the color scheme of antique dolls' houses. The white façade with slate-blue roof offers a simple yet sophisticated contrast to the elaborate interior. All the windows and ledges are highlighted with a cream-colored paint. Commercial windows and doors are used throughout; few would dispute that it is barely worth the effort to make all your own fixtures when there are many readymade styles and qualities to choose from.

Many dolls' houses are positioned on a firm board that lets the house be lifted without being handled.

Constructing the Doll's House

hammer
soft pencil
carpenter's square or T-square
craft knife
jigsaw
keyhole saw
router with ⅜ in. (10 mm) cutter
screwdriver
nail punch

fine-grade sandpaper
measuring tape
electric drill
¹⁄₃₂ in. (1 mm) drill bit
dampened rag for cleaning off excess glue
small 3 in. (7.5 cm) foam paint roller
paint brushes—1 in. (2.5 cm),
½ in. (13 mm) and fine model-painting size for windows
8 x 4 ft (2.4 x 1.2 m) sheet of quality construction board ⅜ in. (10 mm) thick. (Custom board or craftwood is easy to work with; or use exterior-grade ⅜ in. [10 mm] plywood. Check plywood sheet for warping before purchasing. This will give you enough for a base to stand the doll's house on when completed.)
supply of 1 in. (2.5 cm) nails specifically designed for hardwoods which offer a superior grip and excellent join. (Alternatively, use 1 in. [2.5 cm] panel nails.)
white carpenter's glue (PVA) in a squeeze bottle with a fine nozzle
½ in. (13 mm) brass piano hinge of required length
⅜ in. (10 mm) brass screws for the hinge
½ in.-square (13 mm-square) wood strips to reinforce hinged section
⅛ in. (3 mm) wood strip to build out left-hand side wall
box catch for locking door into closed position. (A small antique latch would look good.)
2 wooden clothespins
3–4 lengths of acrylic "wrought iron" commonly available in different styles from a doll's house shop
6 standard 5 x 3½ in. (12.7 x 9 cm) double-hung windows
2 French windows—same width but taller than standard windows
two 3½ x 3½ in. (9 x 9 cm) fixed dormer windows
1 standard-size front door
Note: *If you choose different-sized windows or door, alter the cutting plan to suit.*
white acrylic paint, preferably in a satin finish. (Avoid gloss paints as these detract from the old-world decor.)
acrylic paint—slate blue, terracotta, cream

Lovers of Victoriana who are also woodwork enthusiasts can now make their own Victorian Doll's House.

This simple-to-construct Victorian Doll's House offers plenty of scope for decorating and has a clever front opening that allows for easy access.

Read all the instructions all the way through before starting.

Mark out all the pattern pieces on the wooden sheet, taking great care to keep the angles true and the lines perfectly straight. Mark in all windows, door and stairwell. Double check all the measurements. Label each piece clearly.

Note: The balcony floors are cut from a double thickness of board for the best visual effect. Use scraps to glue and clamp into one thickness before cutting.

Cut out all the pieces, using the jigsaw. Take great care to make straight cuts.

Sand the edges lightly to remove any roughness.

Check the fit of the windows and the door, as these holes often need minor adjustments.

Cut a rabbet (rebate) groove in the back section and the sides as shown to accept the floor.

Prop up the side walls and put in the base and top floor only. Glue and nail these into position. If timber tends to split, pre-drill the nail holes with a $1/32$ in.(1 mm) bit. Clean up any excess glue as you work. Check the angles with the square to make sure the work is still true.

Fit in the two middle floors, glue and nail into position.

Place the back in position and check the angles. Glue and nail into position.

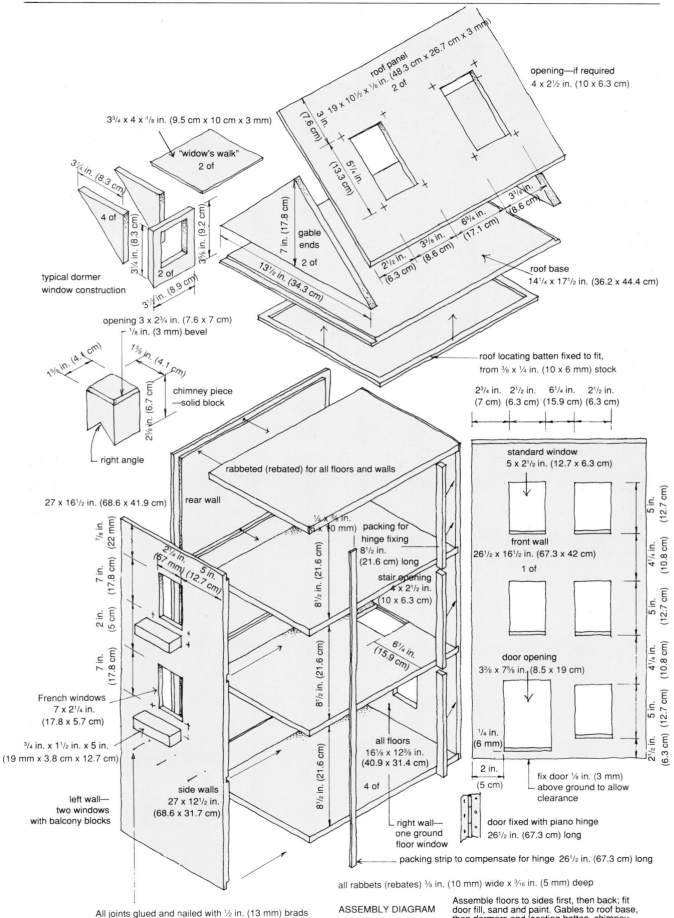

roof panel
19 x 10½ x ⅛ in. (48.3 cm x 26.7 cm x 3 mm)
2 of

opening—if required
4 x 2½ in. (10 x 6.3 cm)

3 in. (7.6 cm)

5¼ in. (13.3 cm)

3⅜ in. (8.6 cm)

6¾ in. (17.1 cm)

3⅜ in. (8.6 cm)

3¾ x 4 x ⅛ in. (9.5 cm x 10 cm x 3 mm)

"widow's walk"
2 of

3¼ in. (8.3 cm)

4 of

3¼ in. (8.3 cm)

3⅝ in. (9.2 cm)

3¼ in. (8.3 cm)

2 of

3½ in. (8.9 cm)

typical dormer
window construction

7 in. (17.8 cm)

gable
ends
2 of

13½ in. (34.3 cm)

2½ in. (6.3 cm)

3⅜ in. (8.6 cm)

roof base
14¼ x 17½ in. (36.2 x 44.4 cm)

opening 3 x 2¾ in. (7.6 x 7 cm)
⅛ in. (3 mm) bevel

1⅝ in. (4.1 cm)

1⅝ in. (4.1 cm)

1⅝ in. (4.1 cm)

chimney piece
—solid block

2⅝ in. (6.7 cm)

right angle

roof locating batten fixed to fit,
from ⅜ x ¼ in. (10 x 6 mm) stock

2¾ in. (7 cm) 2½ in. (6.3 cm) 6¼ in. (15.9 cm) 2½ in. (6.3 cm)

standard window
5 x 2½ in. (12.7 x 6.3 cm)

rabbeted (rebated) for all floors and walls

27 x 16½ in. (68.6 x 41.9 cm)

rear wall

¼ x ⅜ in. (6 x 10 mm)

packing for
hinge fixing
8½ in. (21.6 cm) long

stair opening
4 x 2½ in. (10 x 6.3 cm)

8½ in. (21.6 cm)

6¼ in. (15.9 cm)

front wall
26½ x 16½ in. (67.3 x 42 cm)
1 of

5 in. (12.7 cm)

4¼ in. (10.8 cm)

5 in. (12.7 cm)

4¼ in. (10.8 cm)

5 in. (12.7 cm)

2½ in. (6.3 cm)

⅞ in. (22 mm)

7 in. (17.8 cm)

2¼ in. (57 mm)

5 in. (12.7 cm)

2 in. (5 cm)

7 in. (17.8 cm)

8½ in. (21.6 cm)

8½ in. (21.6 cm)

8½ in. (21.6 cm)

door opening
3⅜ x 7⅝ in. (8.5 x 19 cm)

French windows
7 x 2¼ in. (17.8 x 5.7 cm)

¾ in. x 1½ in. x 5 in. (19 mm x 3.8 cm x 12.7 cm)

left wall—
two windows
with balcony blocks

side walls
27 x 12½ in. (68.6 x 31.7 cm)

all floors
16⅛ x 12⅜ in. (40.9 x 31.4 cm)
4 of

right wall—
one ground
floor window

¼ in. (6 mm)

2 in. (5 cm)

fix door ⅛ in. (3 mm)
above ground to allow
clearance

door fixed with piano hinge
26½ in. (67.3 cm) long

packing strip to compensate for hinge 26½ in. (67.3 cm) long

all rabbets (rebates) ⅜ in. (10 mm) wide x ³⁄₁₆ in. (5 mm) deep

All joints glued and nailed with ½ in. (13 mm) brads
on approximately 3 in. (7.6 cm) centers.

ASSEMBLY DIAGRAM

Assemble floors to sides first, then back; fit
door fill, sand and paint. Gables to roof base,
then dormers and locating batten, chimney
and balcony blocks.

Glue and nail the doorstep into position. This is a single thickness of wood, unlike the balcony and should have its underside flush with the bottom of the front section.

Cut the piano hinge to size and screw to the front section using ⅜ in. (1 cm) screws. Remember that the front opens out from the left-hand side. You will need to reinforce the front right-hand side on the inside of the wall to accommodate the strong screws. Do this with the sections of ½ in. (13 mm) timber. Glue and nail them between the floors against the front corner. It is important to have a strong hinge setup that will take the weight of the front façade "door" without putting undue stress on the walls. In addition, a thin strip of ⅛ in. (3 mm) beading or

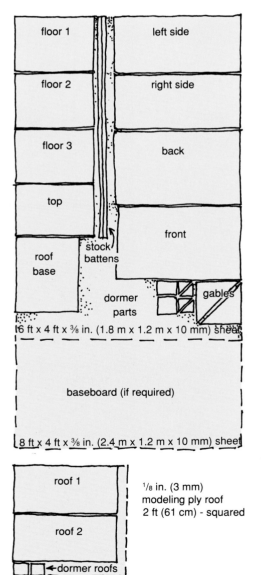

cutting layout

cardboard is needed down the left-hand side to compensate for the thickness of the hinge. Glue into position to avoid a gap when the façade is closed.

Glue the balcony floors into position flush with the window ledge. Turn the house on its side to allow these to dry thoroughly without support.

Make up the roof section including the chimney. Cut the turned ends off the two clothespins to make two 1–1½ in. (2.5–3.8 cm) tall chimney pots. Glue into position.

Sand lightly inside and out. Use a large dry paintbrush to dust off the house inside and out.

Paint the exterior with the white acrylic, using the small foam roller. A roller will give a smoother finish than a brush. The raw boards will need at least two coats.

Paint the roof section and half the chimney with slate-blue paint.

Paint the acrylic "wrought iron" slate blue and then glue to the roof ridge and the balconies.

A quick-drying craft glue is easier to work with for this step. Use generous dobs of glue to fill the corner joins on the balcony rails. When dry, touch up the paintwork with a small brush.

If you wish to stand the doll's house on a baseboard, cut the board to a desired size and decorate as described in the next section.

Screw the box catch onto the left-hand edge of the house.

Paint the windows and front door, taking great care. Avoid using too much paint, as that is harder to control. As you finish the windows, glue them into position lightly in case they need to be removed before all the internal decoration is finished. Hold back on the interior architraving until after papering and painting are completed.

Miniature Topiary Trees

Use these delightful little trees to decorate the front doorstep. They can be redecorated at Christmastime with red bows and tiny red berries for a festive touch.

*1 thin wooden skewer with pointed ends,
or 2 heavy-duty toothpicks
2 woody seedpods of the hard, round sort found in
abundance around the world under such trees as
American sycamores, London planes, buttonwoods*

and other members of genus Platanus *or the spikier ones found under sweetgum, redgum, star-leafed gum and other members of the Liquidambar family.*
acrylic craft paint—terracotta, dull green
2 screw-on style toothpaste lids
quick-drying craft glue
selection of tiny dried flowers
12 in. (30 cm) of 1/16 in. (2 mm) silk ribbon
in desired color

Cut 2 in. (5 cm) from each end of the skewer. Push one pointed end firmly into each seedpod and secure with a dab of glue. Paint the seedpod and the stick with dull green paint and put aside to dry. Paint the two lids with terracotta-colored paint, both inside and out. When the paint dries, glue the sticks upright in the little "pots" using a generous pool of glue. You will need to lean the trees against something firm to maintain a straight position while they dry. When the trees are firm, glue a little garden soil into the top of the pots to hide the glue. Decorate the round head of the "tree" with tiny flowers. Touch them with glue, then push them into the crevices of the seedpod. Incorporate a few loops of fine ribbon to heighten the effect. When the trees are finished, tie a loose silk ribbon bow under each ball. Glue the topiary trees to either side of the doorstep.

Now that the exterior of the doll's house is complete, the decorating can begin. There are many readymade miniature pieces available to furnish your doll's house, but some are more fun to make yourself. The following ideas and patterns will give you a wide knowledge of the techniques used in miniature decorating.

GROUND FLOOR KITCHEN

Specialty miniature shops have a wonderful range of kitchen gadgets and cookware to decorate the kitchen.

The main feature in this kitchen is the fireplace with its kit-form wood stove. Make the fireplace first and position this temporarily before making any decorating decisions. By placing the fireplace on the rear wall you maximize the amount of space available for furniture.

The old-fashioned wood-paneled door is a trick of the trade that is very useful for giving an illusion of depth. The door is nonfunctioning and is simply glued into position. If you decide to wallpaper the kitchen rather than paint it, glue the door onto the wall afterwards for a neat finish.

Flooring is a matter of personal taste and can be varied to suit the style of the house. This floor is polished oak and gives a rich flavor to the kitchen.

The warmth of a Victorian kitchen is displayed complete with cooking utensils and bric-à-brac.

Prepared sheets are available: glue them into position and then stain and polish them. Make sure to glue them into position before securing the fireplace.

When decorating the walls, consider a two-tone color scheme that uses a pretty frieze. This can make a room look larger and is much less expensive than buying two sheets of miniature wallpaper. Any small-print ½ in. (13 mm) wide ribbon glued on the wall will imitate a fancy frieze.

An old-style plate shelf is a simple decorating feature that can look quite authentic. Choose a small square profile of balsa stick that can be glued along the walls at above head height. Paint these strips white before gluing into position.

An old-fashioned sideboard dresser is essential in a Victorian kitchen. The pattern is very simple and an excellent first project for the beginner furniture builder. It is cut from bass wood and simply glued together.

Fireplace

thick cardboard, quick-drying craft glue
small quantity of prepared gap-filler product or a stiff
mixture of white woodworking glue and plaster
balsa sheet for mantelpiece and hearth
wooden skewer, brown shoe polish
matte black acrylic paint, scissors

Enlarge the scaled patterns as instructed on page 4 and cut out the fireplace, flue and fireplace back patterns from the thick card. The flue section that forms the top of the fireplace may need to be cut down to size after the fireplace is completed. Score and fold back the flaps along the dotted line. Glue the back of the fireplace into positon. Fold the flue into shape and glue securely to the top of the fireplace. The flue will sit flush against the back of the kitchen wall. Cut the mantelpiece and hearth from balsa wood. Paint the hearth black and glue onto the prepared floor at the back of the kitchen. Stain the mantelpiece with brown shoe polish and glue into position on top of the fireplace. At this stage, check the overall height of the fireplace by placing in position on the hearth. Trim to size with scissors. Any gaps at the ceiling level will be covered by the cornice. Remove the

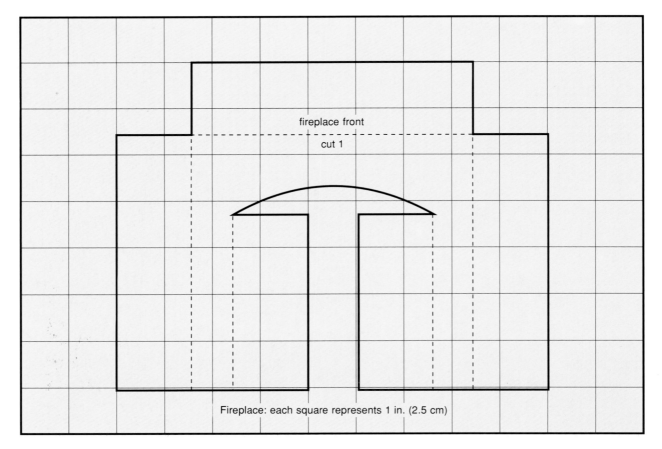

fireplace front

cut 1

Fireplace: each square represents 1 in. (2.5 cm)

fireplace and paint with the gap-filler or plaster mix. Try to use a stucco technique, to leave as much texture as possible: load your brush with the mixture and dab it on. When surface is completely dry, paint the inside of the fireplace black or grey and the outside a color to blend with your color scheme.

Glue the fireplace onto the hearth and flush against the rear wall. A wooden skewer cut to length forms an old-style drying rail just under the mantelpiece. If you wish to hang pans and utensils from the front of the fireplace, glue a strip of stained balsa down each side of the fireplace front.

Sideboard Dresser

This is a long, old-style kitchen dresser that is designed to display those beautiful rows of china

plates and ornaments found in Victorian kitchens. It can be made as a whole or just as a base or wall shelves.

$^1/_{16}$ in. (2 mm) thick fine-grained craft timber. A large range of suitable sheets is available from model-making suppliers and miniature specialists.
sharp razor-toothed saw,
fret saw or miniature sawing table
acrylic paint to finish
quick-drying craft glue
fine sandpaper

Enlarge the scaled patterns as instructed on page 4 and carefully transfer the pattern to the selected timber using the straight edges of the sheet as much as possible to minimize the number of straight cuts.

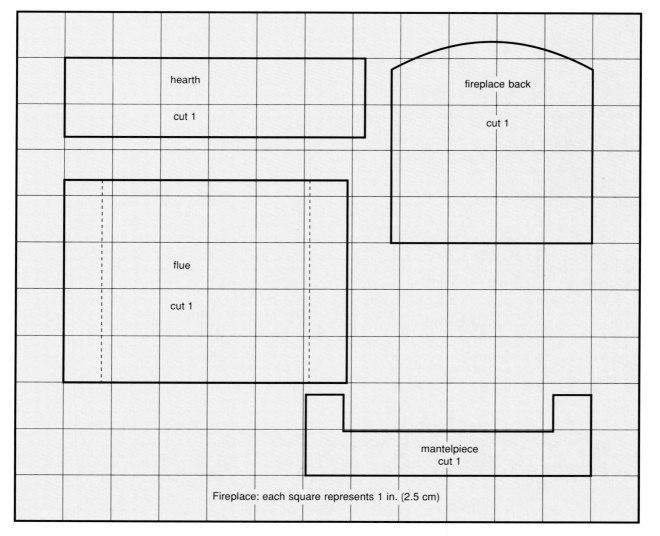

Fireplace: each square represents 1 in. (2.5 cm)

Use the razor-toothed saw to cut out every piece as accurately as possible. Label each piece as it is cut. Sand each piece lightly, smoothing the edges as well. Good curves can be made by wrapping some sandpaper around a pencil to make a curved tool. The top backboard can be scored to resemble 6 in. (15 cm) planks by ruling sharp pencil lines at ½ in. (13 mm) intervals. The paint will eventually emphasize the grooves and cover any pencil marks.

Assemble the top and bottom separately and then glue together. Thin down some artist-quality acrylic paint and paint the dresser in a color to match your kitchen color scheme. Avoid bright modern colors that will detract from the Victorian decor. Add generations of "wear and tear" to your new piece of furniture by painting with a wash of very thin brown watercolor. If you have some narrow old lace, you could add lace fronts to the two plate shelves to represent traditional shelf liners.

Braided Hearth Rug

*three 6 ft (1.8 m) lengths of embroidery floss in
harmonizing colors
needle and white sewing thread
3 rubber bands to secure hanks while braiding*

Knot the three embroidery floss lengths together and wedge the knot in a bureau drawer. Sitting facing the drawer, braid the floss into a firm and even braid. You will find it easier if you roll each thread up into a neat hank and unwind as needed. The more length you braid, the larger your rug will be. To stitch the rug together, start by stitching a straight center of approximately 1½ in. (3.8 cm), so that the spiral that evolves will form an oval shape. Work on the back of the rug, using tiny stitches to pull the two braids together. The work will curl as you progress but can easily be pressed flat when finished. When

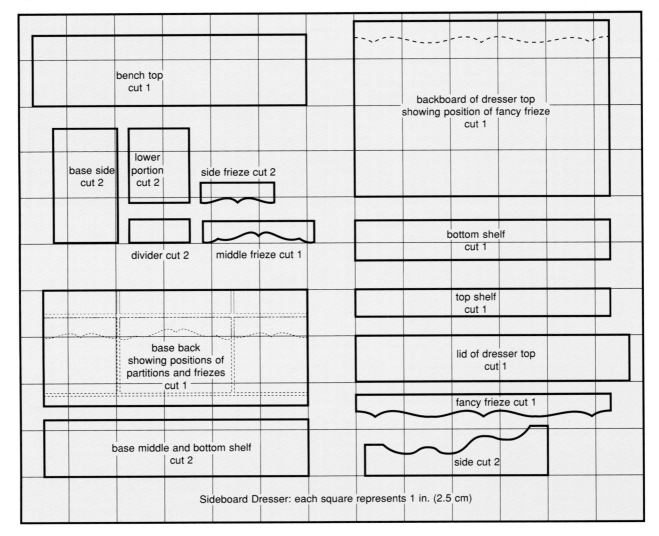

bench top
cut 1

backboard of dresser top
showing position of fancy frieze
cut 1

base side
cut 2

lower
portion
cut 2

side frieze cut 2

bottom shelf
cut 1

divider cut 2 middle frieze cut 1

top shelf
cut 1

base back
showing positions of
partitions and friezes
cut 1

lid of dresser top
cut 1

fancy frieze cut 1

base middle and bottom shelf
cut 2

side cut 2

Sideboard Dresser: each square represents 1 in. (2.5 cm)

you achieve the desired size, cut the braid and stitch the end onto the back of the rug to conceal it. Press with a steam iron.

Feather Duster

1 fancy toothpick with turned end
brown shoe polish
tiny soft feathers trimmed from a real feather duster
quick-drying craft glue
black sewing thread

Cut the toothpick to 1¼ in. (3.2 cm), allowing the shaped end of the toothpick to become the handle of the duster. Stain the handle with the brown shoe polish. Using small pieces of feather, approximately ³/₄ in. (19 mm) long, glue onto the cut end of the toothpick until a brush is formed. After the feathers have dried in position, wind some cotton around the base of the feathers and smear with craft glue to make a strong bind. Hang the duster from a small hook on the fireplace.

Home Sweet Home Sampler

It is very important to work in a small hoop to keep your work from distorting. Ask at your needlework supply shop for the finest counted-stitch fabric that they stock. Work cross stitches with one strand of embroidery floss. When finished, press firmly with a steam iron and glue to light cardboard. When dry, cut cardboard-backed fabric into required size. A simple frame can be made from stained matchsticks.

Acorn Bowls

Little wooden bowls are easily made with acorn cups found all year long under any oak tree. Sand the rough texture from the outside with sandpaper and you have a perfect wooden bowl. Fill a few with dried flowers, tiny seashells or even sesame seeds that will look like miniature almonds.

Seashells

Delightful little seashells are easily found on most beaches at low tide. Collect a few handfuls and use them as the Victorians were fond of doing: display a variety of little shells along a mantelpiece or spare shelf. If you can find a small glass dome, make a pyramid of seashells to display. The small round glass mirrors found in pressed-powder compacts can be used to make shell-edged wall mirrors that look very effective over a fireplace.

Dried Flower Arrangements

A wonderful old-fashioned technique for drying flowers is ideal for drying tiny flowerettes that you can use in miniature flower arrangements. In a small lunchbox-size plastic container, mix ½ cup (4 oz/ 125 g) of borax with ½ cup (4 oz/125 g) of coarse-ground polenta (cornmeal). This mixture is a simple drying environment for any little flowers left embedded in it. After a few days, small flowers will have dried enough to be taken out and gently brushed to remove any powder. Glue into small vases, building

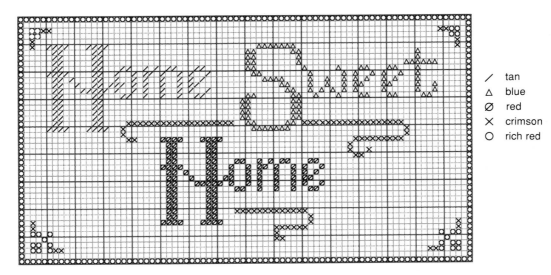

/ tan
△ blue
Ø red
X crimson
O rich red

up pleasing arrangements. Use a small brush and watercolor pigment to color the flowers to the desired shades.

Country Cottage Needlework

Choose the smallest scale of counted-stitch fabric available in order to keep this very small. For instance, Aida cloth with 20 stitches to the inch (2.5 cm) would yield overall dimensions of 2 x 1½ in. (5 x 3.5 cm). The black outline stitches are worked last, and with a single strand. Press and mount onto thin card before framing.

Lace-edged Round Table

The old-fashioned pedestal table in the kitchen is a clever conversion of a cheap plastic table. Many pieces of commercial plastic furniture available for children can be worked over to give superb results. Spray enamels adhere well to plastic and are available in a good range of colors. Two light spray coats are preferable to one heavy coat that may run. When completely dry, glue a strip of old lace around the tabletop. A small lace edge can also be used on any mantelpieces to give that overdecorated look that the Victorian era is noted for.

Concertina Hanging Rack

matchsticks
sharp craft knife
brown shoe polish
quick-drying craft glue

Cut six matchsticks into 1 in. (2.5 cm) lengths. Stain each with brown shoe polish. Glue the sticks into a herringbone pattern with three sticks sloping to the right as a base and three to the left over the top to create the expanded rack. Glue an assortment of kitchen utensils to the rack with the glue.

Rug Beater

12 in. (30.5 cm) very fine wire
pair long-nosed pliers

Use the drawing as a guide to twist the wire into shape. This takes patience but is really quite easy. Fold the wire in half so you are working with a

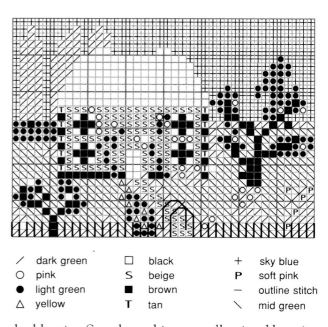

/	dark green	□	black	+	sky blue
O	pink	S	beige	P	soft pink
●	light green	■	brown	—	outline stitch
△	yellow	T	tan	\	mid green

double wire. Start by making a small twisted loop in the middle of the piece and then follow the drawing to make a traditional heart-shaped beater. Make the handle by twisting the two strands together and end the handle by looping the wires back.

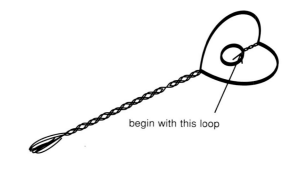

begin with this loop

Hanging Herbs

a few sprigs of small-leaved grasses
cotton thread

Make a tiny bunch of "herbs" and tie the cotton firmly around the stems. Make a long loop to hang the bunch from the ceiling. Make a few bunches, using different grasses to simulate different types of herbs. If these lack fresh green color after drying, give the bunches a light spray with a green florist spray.

Sack of Potatoes

Use tiny sacks for all sorts of bulk foodstuffs. Fill a few bags with cotton wool and tie off the top of the bag to create ears. Label as flour, sugar, etc.

old white handkerchief fabric
white sewing thread and needle
12 tiny potatoes. Shape these of Fimo modeling
material, then roll them in cocoa before cooking in the
oven to give a texture like newly dug potatoes
quick-drying craft glue
scissors, ruler
fine-tipped brown felt pen
weak tea solution for stain

Cut rectangles 1½ x 4 in. (3.5 x 10 cm) from the handkerchief. Fold these in half to form rectangles 1½ x 2 in. (3.5 x 5 cm). Using the folded edge as the bottom of the sack, stitch up the sides with tiny backstitches. Turn the sacks through to the right side and fill with the Fimo potatoes. Glue each potato into place until the sack is overflowing. Turn the top raw edge down a few times for realism. Using the fine-tipped pen, draw a simple company brand on the front of the sack. Stain the white fabric with weak tea solution for a realistically worn look.

Cookies on a Tray

Make variations of the cookies. They will be useful when decorating the dining room and setting the upstairs table for morning tea.

square of thick foil found as seals on beverage cans
red Fimo, off-white Fimo
thick drinking straw, cut in two
scissors, ruler

Cut a square of thick foil ¾ x 1 in. (19 mm x 2.5 cm) to be the baking sheet. Soften the Fimo and roll three pea-sized balls, two off-white and one red. Roll these balls out until they are as thin as possible without tearing when lifted. Sandwich the red layer between the two off-white layers and gently smooth the stack together. Use the thick drinking straw as a cookie cutter. If the tiny cookies stick in the straw, poke each one out with a blunt stick. Arrange the cookies on the miniature baking sheet and follow the Fimo label instructions to harden them.

Use any scraps of the thick foil to create a set of baking pans to put on the shelves in the kitchen. If you wish to ice the tops of your cookies, use a dab of pink acrylic paint mixed with a little PVA glue.

Hanging String of Peppers

red Fimo
needle and cotton thread

Roll out a sausage of red Fimo about ⅛ in. (3 mm) thick. Cut this sausage into small lengths about ¼ in. (6 mm) long. Make as many as you desire. Take each segment and form into a tiny cone shape with one flattened and one slightly pointed end. Cook these on a piece of baking parchment (paper) to avoid sticking. Remove from oven, and when they are just cool enough to handle, use the needle and thread to form a hanging strand of peppers. Hang the string from the mantelpiece.

Lined Cane Basket

These little baskets can be used all over the house for a nostalgic feeling.

cotton-tipped swab stick
quick-drying craft glue
small sharp scissors
scrap of silk fabric
tiny cane basket—commonly found in craft shops or
specialty doll's house suppliers
small length of co-ordinating silk ribbon
¼ in. (6 mm) wide

Use the tip of the cotton swab to smear a fine layer of craft glue over the entire inside surface of the basket. Cut a rough circle of silk that will cover the inside of the basket, and gently push into place. Try to create even folds of excess fabric up the inside. When dry, trim the fabric flush with the top of the basket. Glue a strip of silk ribbon around the top edge, gently easing it around the curved surface. Make two tiny silk ribbon bows to glue each side of the handle. Fill with tiny treasures.

THE DINING ROOM

An elaborately set table and a cosy fireplace are the main features of this room. The heritage color scheme is easily reproduced with a little care. There are many beautiful staircase kits available; they range from very ornate to simple treads. Try to select a staircase that will harmonize with the era and stain the woodwork to suit the decor of the room.

The dining room of the Doll's House presents an inviting scene with its beautifully laid table ready for dinner.

The Floor

Wall-to-wall carpet is a reasonably new phenomenon and not recommended in this period doll's house. Wooden floors with needlepoint rugs look wonderful and offer a lot of flexibility when furnishing. Another alternative, suitable for custom board, is to paint the floor and decorate the edges. This house has an Amish blue floor with a 2 in. (5 cm) border of rose-patterned ribbon glued to the floor. Avoid bulky ribbons as they will not give the right effect. If you enjoy stenciling, you could do this around the edges.

Wallpapering

All doll's house enthusiasts have their own techniques for wallpapering a room. Some are more successful than others. The basic rule is to avoid getting the miniature wallpaper too wet, as this leads to bubbling and creases. A spray-on photographic glue that gives good adhesion with minimum moisture is recommended by many. If you use this technique, spray the pre-measured cut paper, position it on the wall and rub it with a soft rag. Fold creases for any corners before putting the paper into position, to make true straight corners. Any shortcomings at the floor level can be covered by the skirting board, and likewise a fine 1/4 in. (6 mm) half-round molding will serve as a cornice and hide any gaps. These rooms require two sheets of commercial doll's house wallpaper.

Victorian Armchair

thick cardboard, quick-drying craft glue
light card such as an old greeting card
small piece of soft dressmaking velvet
small piece batting (wadding)
4 small black wooden beads
8 in. (20 cm) of scallop-edged lace
24 in. (61 cm) fine braid or gimp

Transfer all the pattern pieces except the back onto the strong cardboard and carefully cut out. Cut the back pattern piece from the greeting card — this will need to curve gently when covered. Start with the side pieces and cover them, inside and out, with velvet. When the glue is dry, trim the velvet to the exact size of the cardboard. The raw edges will be covered with braid when assembled. Cover one seat piece with the velvet, allowing a 1/4 in. (6 mm) turn-under. Repeat with the other seat piece, but pad the top of the card first with batting (wadding) before covering with fabric. This will be the top of the seat. The back section, made from the light card, needs to be covered front and back and the excess fabric trimmed away. Glue the unpadded seat section between the two sides where indicated on the pattern: the wrong side should face upwards, to be covered later by the padded section. Glue on the back of the chair, aligning the top corners first. After the chair has dried, trim the back to fit flush with the sides. Glue on the padded seat section. Glue the beads onto the corners of the base for legs. Glue on the scalloped lace to act as a skirt covering the legs. Trim all raw edges with fine braid.

Rose Hearth Rug

This is a small rug ideal for placing in front of the fireplace. Work with full strands of embroidery threads in cross-stitch for a heavier look. A simple technique for finishing off a small area rug is to coat the back with a generous layer of glue and attach to a scrap of fabric. When dry, cut the excess cloth away from the last row of stitches leaving about 1/8 in. (3 mm) as a border. (This technique is not suitable for large pieces of needlework, which need to be correctly blocked and bound before using as a carpet.) Cut a strip of 1/2 in. (13 mm) grosgrain ribbon down the center and fray it back almost to the selvage. This will give you perfect fringing for the floor rugs:

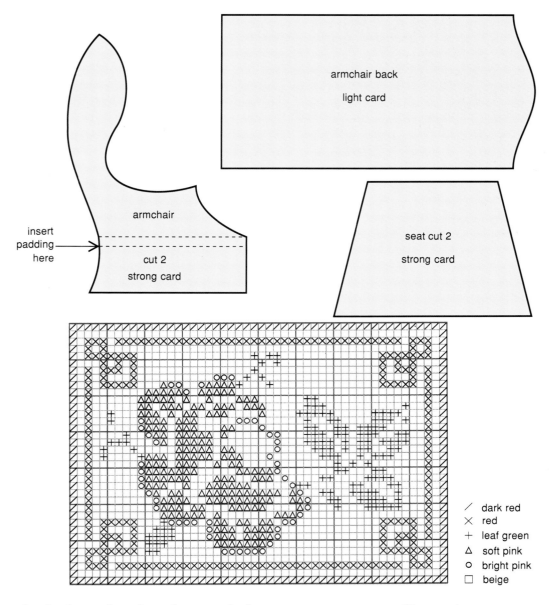

insert
padding
here

armchair

cut 2
strong card

armchair back

light card

seat cut 2

strong card

/ dark red
× red
+ leaf green
△ soft pink
○ bright pink
□ beige

it can be glued into place, butted against the last row of stitches.

Gold Filigree Picture Frames

A simple technique for making ornate frames that can be made to the required size is borrowed from an old Victorian craft. Snippets of lace are cut and glued to light cardboard to form a border. For example, if an oval frame is needed, draw the oval onto some card and glue a symmetrical arrangement around this line. When the border is finished, give the card a number of coats of gold spray paint. Cut any excess card away from the stiff gold lace and mount the artwork in the center. Some motifs worked in guipure lace are suitable as frames in themselves.

Flower Arrangements

The dining room has many opportunities for floral arrangements. Buy a few large cut-crystal beads from a costume supply shop. Mount each bead onto a circle of clear plastic about $1/2$ in. (13 mm) in diameter. This stiff plastic will be invisible to most eyes and provide stability for your flower arrangements. Fill the crystal vases with flowers that you have collected and dried. (This technique is described in the kitchen section.) A good trick to gain height in these arrangements is to cut a $1\frac{1}{2}$ in. (3.8 cm) piece of green-colored pipe cleaner and force this into the hole in the bead. By gluing grasses and flowers to the pipe cleaner, you can gradually build up formal arrangements that have the strength of the hidden wire.

Painted Tray

Oversized serving trays were French in origin and much loved by the Victorian hostess. They were remarkably light, being made from layers of papier mâché, but very strong. They were decorated with a high-gloss black background to imitate the lacquerware that was being imported from the Orient.

Cut thick cardboard as accurately as possible to form the trays. Sand the edges to give very smooth curves. Give both front and back a base coat of black enamel paint. Allow to dry thoroughly. Trace the pattern and transfer the design onto the tray using white graphite paper. Use a very fine brush or a toothpick to paint the design in rich jewel-like colors. Paint tiny scrolls in gold around the outside edge. Use the side of the brush to add a line of gold around the edge of the tray. When completely dry, spray lightly with gloss sealer. As these trays were large and awkward to display on a shelf, they were usually hung by a leather strap from a picture hook.

Needlework Silhouettes

Fancy silhouettes were immensely popular during the Victorian era. They were usually worked in black on white backgrounds. These small pieces look best as a pair and are really an easy project to work on.

small piece of even-weave cloth approx. 20 squares to the inch (8 squares to the centimeter)
black embroidery floss
No. 22 tapestry needle
small embroidery hoop
spray adhesive, thin cardboard, iron

Work both portraits on the same piece of cloth, leaving a gap of at least 1 in. (2.5 cm) between the two borders. The design can be worked with one strand of embroidery floss, to avoid bulkiness. The designs are worked in cross stitch. When the stitching is completed, remove the fabric from the frame and press with a warm iron. Use the spray adhesive to glue the fabric to the thin cardboard and mount in a suitable frame. Ornate brooch findings can provide tiny picture frames for your needlework and paintings.

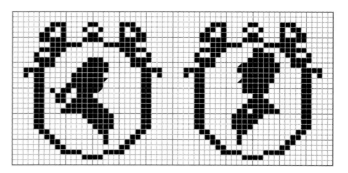

THE UPSTAIRS BEDROOM

This beautiful large room is ideally suited to a main bedroom with a sitting area. You could easily decorate a nursery corner and add a small cradle or baby table full of paraphernalia. This is the place to use lots of dainty lace and fine trimmings. Remember that this era was characterized by overdecoration and adornment.

Bed with Canopy

Many beautiful beds are available through miniature suppliers. This bedroom is graced with an elegant

four-poster that is simply constructed from an inexpensive kit. The bed was finished with a high-gloss cedar-colored varnish that suits the rich tones of the bedroom.

Dressing of the bed can be as elaborate or simple as you wish. By keeping to whites and creams, you can change the decor of the room and still maintain the same bed linen.

To make the mattress, you will need a rectangle of foam ³/₄ in. (19 mm) thick cut to the appropriate size. (Often thick kitchen sponges can be found close to the correct size.) When the foam is cut it can be very neatly wrapped like a parcel, with quick-drying craft glue securing the flaps on the underside. Old mattresses were most often covered with stiff unbleached cotton fabric or black-and-white striped ticking. To imitate this, you could use unbleached calico and draw on stripes with a permanent marker.

Sheets and pillowcases are easily made from old white handkerchiefs. These are easily found in second-hand shops, often with hand-made lace borders that will look beautiful as bed sheets. Tiny pillowcases should be made from the same fine fabric. Make generous-sized pillows that should look a little overstuffed compared to the modern pillow. Sew together two rectangles cut to size, leaving the end open to turn through. Stuff with teased-out cotton wool and sew up the opening with tiny slip stitches. Frills of very fine gathered lace can be stitched around the edges for a sophisticated look.

Round satin pillows are easily made from ³/₄ in. (19 mm) satin or silk ribbon. Choose ribbon that is either very soft or well washed, so that it gathers up into soft, close folds. Cut a small length and stitch along one edge with tiny running stitches; gather these up to form a tight rosette. Repeat with another strip and join the two rosettes together around the outside edge with small whip stitches. Edge with very fine lace if desired.

The coverlet needs to look sumptuous and well tailored. A visit to the local antique shop that deals in old laces is well worth the effort. You need only a small panel of quality lace to give your bed that heirloom atmosphere. A damaged piece of lace could be cut into the appropriate size. Slip stitch the lace panel at the bottom corners to sit neatly. Avoid new shiny laces that will detract from the old-world feel of the room.

The perfect Victorian bedroom with its exquisite lace-canopy bed, red velvet chaise longue, floral wallpaper, draped boudoir table and miniature floral wreath and topiary balls.

A bolster cushion across the back of the bed is easily made by covering a small length of thick dowel with padding and then a tube-shaped pillowslip. Gather the ends of the fabric tube to form tight rosettes; tie off with a firm knot. If your bed needs a dust ruffle around the base, slip stitch scalloped lace to the coverlet after the bed is made. Old crochet laces are heavy enough to drape well in this project.

The canopy can be made using fine tulle or fancy pre-gathered lace to form a valance. Avoid over-dressing the canopy, as this could detract from the base and look too heavy.

Draped Boudoir Table

1 disposable foam drinking cup
cardboard circle 2 in. (5 cm) in diameter
scraps of old lace for edging
quick-drying craft glue, dressmaking pins
circle of soft dressmaking velvet 6 ³/₄ in.
(17 cm) in diameter

Cut the foam cup down to approximately 2¼ in. (5.7 cm) in height. Turn the cup over and glue the cardboard circle to the bottom. If you wish to have a lace edging on the velvet skirt, glue a lace strip around the circumference of the velvet piece. Next, glue the center of the cloth onto the cardboard circle using a minimum of glue. Run a line of glue around the lower section of the cup and gently coax the fabric into soft folds against the cup. Secure the folds with dressmaking pins if necessary while drying. Cut a 3 in. (7.6 cm) square from an old lace panel and glue this over the tabletop for an extra cloth.

Miniature Books

A collection of tiny books can be positioned around the house. Cut small rectangles approximately $1/2$ x $5/8$ in. (13 x 16 mm) and smaller from thick cardboard. Paint the edges gold and allow to dry. These become the pages of the book. Cover with a sleeve of dark-colored paper slightly larger than the pages. Add a few fine gold lines to the spine for effect.

Envelopes and Papers

Find some very fine paper, such as an airmail envelope, and transfer the pattern to make as many as you desire.

Cut and fold the little envelopes. Secure the bottom three flaps with a tiny dab of glue applied with a toothpick. Make matching sheets of paper by cutting rectangles $1/2$ x $1/8$ in. (13 x 3 mm) from the same fine paper. A fountain pen can be whittled from the rounded end of a toothpick. Make a thin capsule shape about $1/2$ in. (13 mm) long and paint it navy blue. When dry, paint a very fine gold line around the pen to denote the top and bottom. Cut a $1/8$ in. (3 mm) piece from a single staple and glue this into position for the pocket grip. Glue the pen onto a piece of paper so it is not easily lost. Tie bundles of envelopes together with a single strand of matching embroidery floss and display with the paper and pen.

Tapestry Arabian Slippers

tiny scrap of fine black leather or vinyl
tiny scrap of red satin—ribbon would suffice
embroidery floss in several colors
quick-drying craft glue
very fine even-weave fabric or canvas (#27 count is preferable)

Using three strands of black, grey and red embroidery floss, make a braid that will be the trim around the slippers. If the braid looks too bulky, split the threads to give a finer trim. Braid about 6 in. (15 cm) of trim and put aside.

Cut two small soles from the leather, using the pattern below as a guide. Smear the wrong sides of both the soles with glue and cover with the red satin. Following the shape of the sole, trim away excess satin. The next step is to stitch the fronts of the slippers using only two strands of floss. Embroider with continental stitch.

When stitching is finished, smear the back of the work with glue and allow to dry thoroughly. Use the scissors to trim around the tapestry as close as possible without cutting the stitches. Glue the curved section to the front of the sole. When dry, glue the trim around the edge of the soles, keeping the join at the heel end of the sole. Glue the trim over the top of the slipper to hide the raw edge.

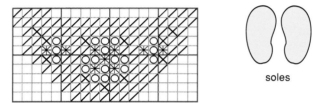

soles

/ cream O bright pink ✳ soft pink X leaf green

Hat Box

thin cardboard—such as greeting card
fine cotton fabric with small print
thin braid trim or silk ribbon
quick-drying craft glue, gold paint

Trace the pattern and cut out the lid and base as accurately as possible. Smear a small section of the fabric with glue and firmly press the card onto this. Weight the card as it dries to avoid distortion. When dry, trim the fabric flush with the card pattern (the coating of glue should prevent fraying). Make sharp folds along the dotted lines and carefully glue the sides together. When dry, paint the inside of the lid and base with gold paint. Trim around the edge of the lid with fine braid or ribbon to hide the unavoidable untidiness. Decorate your hat box with ribbons and bows. Make a few of these to stack on shelves or on top of the wardrobe.

Wastepaper Bin

thin cardboard—such as greeting card
gold paint, 4 in. (10 cm) fine lace
quick-drying craft glue

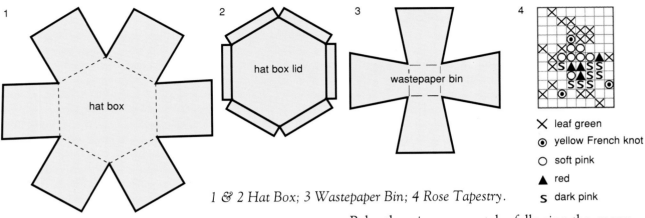

1 hat box	2 hat box lid	3 wastepaper bin	4 Rose Tapestry

1 & 2 Hat Box; 3 Wastepaper Bin; 4 Rose Tapestry.

X leaf green
⊙ yellow French knot
○ soft pink
▲ red
S dark pink

Trace the pattern onto cardboard and cut out carefully. Make sharp folds along the dotted lines by scoring first with a sharp point. Join the sides with a minimum of glue. Paint the bin inside and out with gold paint. Finish the bin with a trim of fine lace on the top edge. Tear up a few pieces of tissue as realistic litter to put in the bin.

Topiary Ball

Hang the topiary ball from the bed to add floral charm to the room by following the instructions for making the Topiary Tree balls (page 16) but use a mixture of pink ribbons and pink flowers. Hang from a long loop of fine pink silk ribbon.

Jointed Teddy Bear

pale brown Fimo
toothpick, silk ribbon for bow tie, thin metal skewer
bead wire, four tiny clear glass beads
black enamel paint for detailing

Refer to the drawing to determine proportions and shape of the teddy bear. Make a jelly-bean-shaped body approximately ³/₄ in. (19 mm) long. Roll a pea-sized ball for the head and join to the top of the body. Gently squeeze the front of the head to form a snout. Flatten two tiny balls of Fimo to form the ears and press onto the head. Sculpt fat arms and legs with curved "sausages" about ½ in. (13 mm) long. Flatten the bottoms of the legs to form paw pads. Press arms and legs temporarily into place on the body and make a hole with the thin metal skewer through "arm-body-arm" and "leg-body-leg."

Bake the pieces separately, following the manufacturer's instructions. When cool, assemble using diagram 1 as a guide. Thread the arms and legs to the body using the bead wire and secure the ends with the tiny glass beads. Paint small facial features, using the point of a toothpick to achieve a fine dot for each eye. The nose should be an inverted triangle shape with a fine line for the classic teddy bear mouth. Add a tiny silk ribbon bow tie.

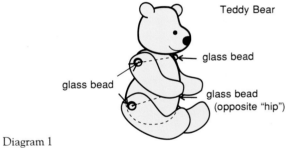

Teddy Bear
glass bead
glass bead
glass bead
(opposite "hip")

Diagram 1

Simple Rose Tapestry

fine white fabric—an old white handkerchief is
excellent, embroidery floss in five colors
fine needle, white card
old brooch finding—a small oval shape would be
suitable

Improvise an embroidery hoop by using an egg ring and a rubber band. Using one strand of each color, follow the graph and make tiny cross-stitches in approximate positions.

Keep your stitches as small as possible and mistakes will be hardly noticeable. Trim the floss from the back of the work after the stitching has been completed. Glue the fabric to the white card and mount inside the fancy brooch finding.

You can use this pattern to make a petit point lid for a hat box. Add a little padding between fabric and lid before gluing into position.

Victorian Tapestry Doll

19 ¾ in. (50 cm) of 14 count tapestry canvas
18 in. (46 cm) tapestry frame (optional)
needle and colored thread for basting
No. 22 tapestry needle
pins
12 in. (30 cm) of velvet
scissors
toy stuffing
tapestry yarns–as listed below

Color legend and DMC Tapestry wools needed: numbers in ( ) indicate number of skeins used.

☒	7781	Darkest Straw (1)
☑	7494	Dark Straw (1)
⊟	7473	Medium Straw (2)
Ⅱ	7472	Light Straw (1)
6	7469	Dark Brown (1)
U	7525	Medium Brown
▣	Black	Black (1)
⋮	Blanc	White (1)
◤	7758	Dark Dusky Pink (1)
◣	7760	Light Pink (1)
◆	7950	Dark Flesh (1)
⊡	7162	Light Flesh (1)
▣	7375	Dark Plum (2)
�﹨	7228	Light Plum (1)
◪	7243	Dark Purple (1)
◿	7241	Medium Purple (1)
✛	7715	Light Purple (1)
◤	7226	Dark Pink (1)
◉	7253	Medium Pink (3)
☐	7251	Light Pink (5)
◎	7260	Lightest Pink (1)
◢	7367	Dark Green (1)
◨	7547	Medium Green (1)
⑦	7783	Medium Gold (1)
⊡	7784	Light Gold (1)
⑤	Same color as backing velvet	

* The graph indicates a border of color that can match the backing velvet—this is optional. If stitched, it will make the process of stitching the backing fabric on a little easier .

Back stitch (1 strand)
  Hands—Medium Brown 7525
  Eyes—Dark Brown 7469
  Daffodils—Medium Brown 7525
  Lace—Purple 7243

Embroidery stitches used:
  basketweave
  continental

Preparation

Find the center lines of the tapestry canvas and stitch a basting thread horizontally and vertically the full length.

The canvas can be attached to a tapestry frame to help avoid distortion during the stitching. Attach the tapestry canvas to the tapes on the bar of the tapestry frame by hand stitching with a basting thread, then roll both bars until the canvas is evenly distributed on both sides and tension is firm. Tighten the wing nuts to secure.

If you do not wish to use a tapestry frame, you will more than likely need to block and stretch the completed work. You can make a blocking board by covering a piece of wood larger than the canvas with a sheet of blotting paper or white cloth and placing a sheet of clean graph paper on top.

Place the tapestry face down on the graph paper and, using rustproof drawing pins, pin one edge of the tapestry to the board using the graph lines as a guide to make sure the edges are straight. Place pins about 1½ in. (4 cm) away from the tapestry, spacing pins every inch (2.5 cm) and gently pulling the edges of the canvas into alignment as you pin.

By the time you get to the second edge it may be a bit harder to pull the work into alignment, so dampen the tapestry with water (this softens the sizing on the canvas) and pull and pin the remaining edges of the canvas. Leave the dampened tapestry pinned in position on the board until completely dry. Do not try to hasten the drying with heat. Remove the work from the board when completely dried. If the work is not blocked to your satisfaction, repeat the process.

Little girls played with Victorian tapestry dolls just like this one.

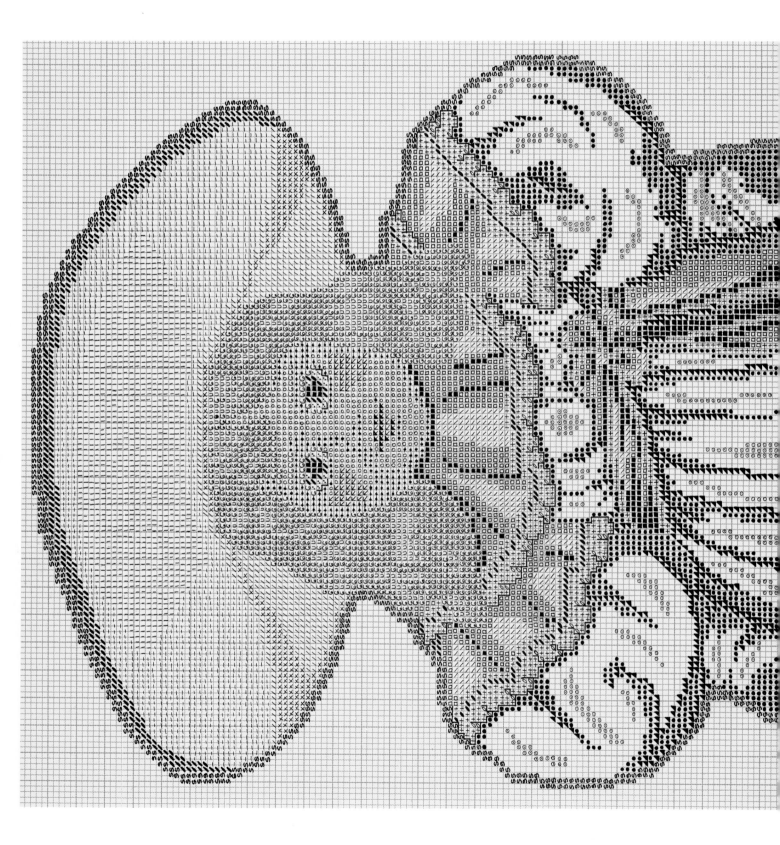

Stitching and Finishing

Following the color legend, match the center of the chart to the center of the tapestry canvas and begin to stitch the design. Refer to the stitch glossary for instructions for basketweave and continental stitches.

To secure yarn for first few stitches in the canvas (see diagram 1—Blind Knot), knot the end of the yarn and insert the needle through the front of the canvas about 2 in. (5 cm) from the starting point.

Diagram 1

Bring the needle through from the back of the canvas at the starting point and work the first stitch (note that the knot is on the front of the work). Continue working the design until the stitching is close to the knot, clip the knot off and continue stitching—the length of yarn on the back of the work has now been secured by stitches worked over it. This should be the only time you will use a knot.

To start and finish off further strands of yarn (see diagram 2) run the needle and yarn under 8 to 10 stitches at the back of the work, then clip the tail.

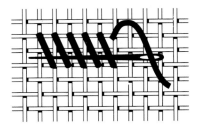

Diagram 2

Do not leave unclipped tails at the back of the work, as these can be pulled through to the front of the work by subsequent stitches and spoil the appearance. Try to avoid starting and finishing the yarn in the same place on the work, as this could make these areas ridged and uneven.

After the tapestry is completed, make up the doll by trimming the canvas back to ⅜ in. (10 mm) from the edge of the stitching. Cut a piece of velvet to the same size.

Lay the velvet and the stitched tapestry right sides together and pin securely. Stitch the two pieces together leaving a 4 in. (10 cm) opening at the bottom. Turn right sides out. Stuff firmly with the toy filling and slip-stitch the opening closed.

Peerless sewing machine (circa 1880) with assorted antique sewing elements.

Heirloom Sewn Church Doll

The tradition of the church doll stems from less hurried times when almost everyone—including the children—went to church on Sunday morning. To make sure they did not disturb the congregation, little girls were encouraged to take along a pretty, soft doll: small enough to fit in a pocket or purse and, if dropped, soft enough to make no noise.

15 ¾ x 18 ⅞ in. (40 x 48 cm) piece of Thai silk
scissors
No. 9 crewel embroidery needle
small quantity of stranded floss for embroidering
facial features
tape measure
soft lead pencil
DMC Stranded Floss: 224, 225, 524
No. 9 milliner's/straw embroidery needle
small amount of toy filling or batting (wadding)
quilting thread
12 in. (30 cm) of 1½ in. (3.8 cm) wide lace edging
9 ⅞ in. (25 cm) of ⅟₃₂ in. (1 mm) wide entredeux
9 ⅞ in. (25 cm) of ⅝ in. (15 mm) wide lace edging
4 ⅞ in. (12.5 cm) of ¼ in. (6 mm) wide lace beading
9 ⅞ x 2 ¾ in. (25 x 7 cm) piece of Thai silk
63 in. (1.6 m) of ⅛ in. (3 mm) wide silk ribbon

Embroidery stitches used:
bullion stitch
lazy daisy
feather stitch
satin stitch

Round off the corners at one end of the 15 ¾ x 18 ⅞ in. (40 x 48 cm) piece of fabric. Working at the same end of the fabric, embroider the facial features with the colored floss, using a satin stitch (see diagram 1).

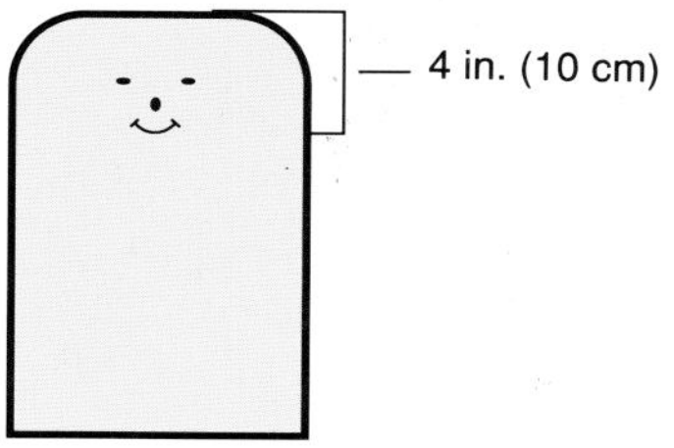

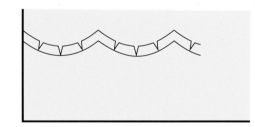

— 4 in. (10 cm)

Diagram 1

At the opposite end of the fabric, measure along the bottom edge of the hem and put a small mark every 2 ⅜ in. (6 cm). This will give you eight sections. The depth of each scallop is ⅝ in. (16 mm). Mark the center of each section with a soft lead pencil and draw in a curved line in each section (see diagram 2).

Cut out the scallops along the marked pencil lines. Measure a ³⁄₁₆ in. (5 mm) hem and turn up; tack along the lower edge (see diagram 3).

Diagram 3

Carefully clip the inner edge of each scallop to measure ³⁄₁₆ in. (5 mm) (see diagram 4).

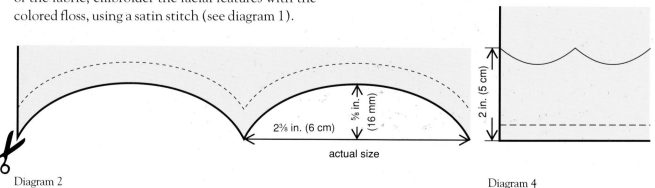

2 ⅜ in. (6 cm)
⅝ in. (16 mm)
actual size
2 in. (5 cm)

Diagram 2

Diagram 4

*The tradition of the Church Doll stems from less hurried times, when everyone
—including the children—went to church on a Sunday morning.*

Turn under the ³⁄₁₆ in. (5 mm) clipped edge and tack in place.

Working on the right side of the fabric and referring to diagram 5, feather stitch over the edge of the hem to hold it in place, using two strands of DMC 225, and embroider the bullion roses with one strand of DMC 224 and lazy daisy leaves with one strand of DMC 524 above the points of the middle five scallops, using the milliner's/straw needle.

Diagram 5

Fold the top edge of the fabric down 4 in. (10 cm). Place a ball of toy filling behind the face (diagram 6) and wrap doubled quilting thread around the fabric at the base of the face to form a neck (diagram 7).

Diagram 6

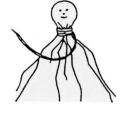

Diagram 7

Wrap several times and secure at the back with a knot. Smooth all the wrinkles from the face by pulling the fabric down from the neck.

Fold the two sides to the back (diagram 8).

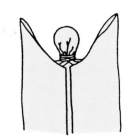

Diagram 8

Refer to diagrams 9 to 15 to form the arms. When you have folded the knot pull and adjust the fabric until the folds resemble an arm in shape. The corner of the fabric that has been pulled through the knot becomes the hand.

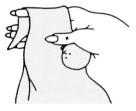

Diagram 9

Diagram 10

Diagram 11

edge of one of the lengths of entredeux. Trim the other side and whip the lace beading to it. Whip the trimmed edge of the entredeux to the other side of the lace beading and trim the other edge. Gather the 9⅞ x 2¾ in. (25 x 7 cm) piece of fabric to 4⅞ in. (12.4 cm) and attach to the trimmed edge of the entredeux (refer to diagram 16 for correct placement).

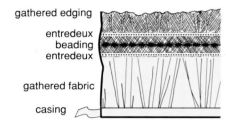

Diagram 16

Make a small casing at the other end, thread the ⅛ in. (3 mm) ribbon through, pull up and tie with a small bow. Attach ribbons to each side of the bonnet as ties (see diagram 17).

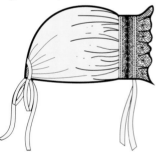

Diagram 17

Diagram 12

Diagram 13

Diagram 14

Diagram 15

Gather the 12 in. (30 cm) length of 1½ in. (3.8 cm) lace edging and attach around the neck as a collar. Cut the entredeux into two equal lengths of 4⅞ in. (12.4 cm) and trim one side of each. Gather the ⅝ in. (16 mm) wide lace edging to 4⅞ in. (12.4 cm) in length and whip to the trimmed

Church Doll

Pop-up Jester

heavyweight paper and pencil
scissors
8 x 8 in. (20 x 20 cm) felt pieces—light blue,
lime green, apricot, peppermint green, mauve, pink,
crimson, dark red and grey
needle and sewing thread
iron for pressing
9 small gold bells
20 in. (50 cm) length of ¼ in. (6 mm) wood dowel
39 in. (1 m) of ⅜ in. (10 mm) wide blue ribbon
quick-drying craft glue or hot-melt glue gun
39 in. (1 m) of ¼ in. (6 mm) wide gold ribbon
1⅝ in. (4 cm) natural wood macramé bead
6-sheet thickness cardboard
20 in. (50 cm) of ¼ in. (6 mm) wide royal blue
velvet ribbon
all-purpose sealer
tracing (graphite) paper
acrylic paint—yellow oxide, white, pale pink, light
brown, light blue, orange, black
polyurethane satin varnish
suitable paint brushes

Embroidery stitches used:
blanket stitch

Trace the diamond pattern (diagram 1) onto the heavyweight paper and cut out to use for a template. Following the list below, use the template to cut felt diamonds from each of the different colors of felt.

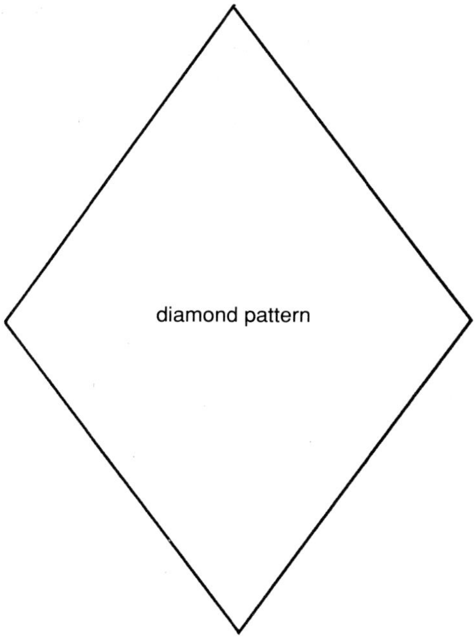

TOP PIECE

◊ mauve—5 diamonds

◊ pink—3½ diamonds

◊ crimson—4 diamonds

◊ dark red—4 diamonds

◊ grey—4 diamonds

diamond pattern

Diagram 1

CONE

◊ light blue—5 diamonds

◊ lime green—3 diamonds

◊ apricot—5 diamonds

◊ peppermint green—6 diamonds

By referring to the color guide for the top piece (diagram 2), carefully position the felt diamonds, in the correct order. Then, with right sides together, neatly blanket stitch them together.

Do the same for the remaining felt diamonds, referring to the color guide given for the cone (diagram 3).

When you have completed the stitching, press the two pieced sections with the iron.

Fold each section in half, right sides together, and blanket stitch the side seams together to form a cone shape and a cylinder shape (diagram 4). Turn both pieces right side out.

*The Pop-up Jester delighted many a Victorian child, with its cheeky hand-painted face,
jingling gold bells and colorful diamond-patterned casing.*

Color Guide for the Top Piece

Diagram 2

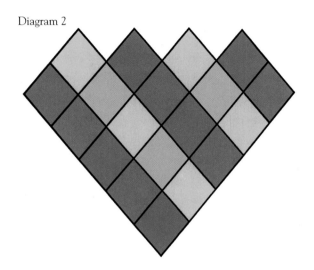

Color Guide for the Cone

Diagram 3

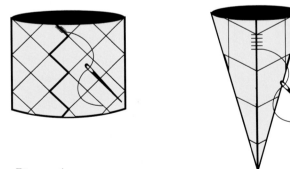

Diagram 4

Transfer the neck frill pattern onto paper and cut from the peppermint green felt. Stitch a small gold bell to each point.

Glue one end of the ⅜ in. (10 mm) wide blue ribbon onto one end of the wood dowel, and neatly wind the ribbon around, overlapping slightly to cover the dowel completely. Glue at the other end to hold.

Attach the ¼ in. (6 mm) gold ribbon at the same end and wind around the dowel leaving a ¼ in. (6 mm) gap between the turns to show the blue ribbon underneath.

Glue the macramé bead onto one end of the dowel. Push the bead up inside the headpiece and into position at the cut-out circle (face opening). Apply a small amount of glue to the inside felt edge of the face opening to stick the felt to the bead.

Gather in the bottom of the headpiece using a running stitch ³⁄₁₆ in. (5 mm) from the bottom edge and pull in tight to fit the dowel (refer to diagram 5).

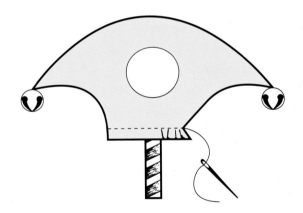

Diagram 5

Next, gather the neck frill along the straight edge and pull up to fit around the dowel underneath the headpiece. Apply a small amount of glue to attach the neck frill to the headpiece.

Transfer the cone pattern onto the thick cardboard and cut out. Form the cone by overlapping the straight edges until the larger end measures 4¾ in. (12 cm) in diameter across the opening and glue in place.

Slip the felt cone shape over the cardboard cone. Pull the edges of the felt at the wider end tightly over onto the inside of the cardboard cone and glue to hold. Set aside to dry.

Transfer the head piece pattern onto paper and cut out from the mauve felt. Fold the head piece in half lengthwise with the right sides together, matching A to C and B to D, and blanket stitch the sides together. Turn to the right side and stitch a small gold bell to each end of the head piece (diagram 5).

Gather the felt cylinder top piece along one edge and pull up the thread to fit around the dowel. Slide it up the dowel and glue to hold in place under the neck frill.

Snip a small hole in the pointed end of the now stiffened felt cone, just large enough to fit the dowel through. Insert the dowel in such a way that the wide mouth of the cone faces upward toward the jester's head.

Glue the lower end of the felt cylinder onto the top edge of the cone, overlapping it by approximately ¼ in. (6 mm).

Glue the ¼ in. (6 mm) royal blue velvet ribbon around the top edge of the cone to hide the join with the top piece and around the hole at the bottom edge of the cone, being sure the dowel can slide through.

Painting the Jester's Face

Seal the macramé bead with all-purpose sealer before painting. Transfer the design (diagram 6) lightly onto the face using the graphite paper. Give the hair

Diagram 6

a base coat of yellow oxide, use white for the eye sockets and pale pink for the lips.

Add a light float of light brown around the outer edge of the face, under the bottom lip, at the corners of the mouth, on the end of the nose and above the eyes—see illustration 1.

Paint the eyes with light blue. Float over the top of the eyes a mixture of light brown and orange.

Use the same color to float over the cheeks, deepening the color slowly at the bottom of the cheeks—see illustration 2.

Wash over the cheeks with pale pink. Paint fine linework with orange around the eyes and at the base of the nose.

Paint light brown linework on the hair, mouth line, around the eyes, around the iris and on the eyebrows. Paint the pupils with black. Paint white highlights in the eyes and on the bottom lip. Refer to illustration 3.

Apply two coats of polyurethane satin varnish to the face to complete.

Leave the Pop-up Jester to dry properly before testing it. To make it work, simply hold the cone with one hand and pull the dowel down with your other hand so that the jester's head slips inside the cone; then pull the cone down and the jester's head pops up!

Illustration 1   Illustration 2   Illustration 3

This little boy waits in anticipation to reveal the Pop-up Jester.

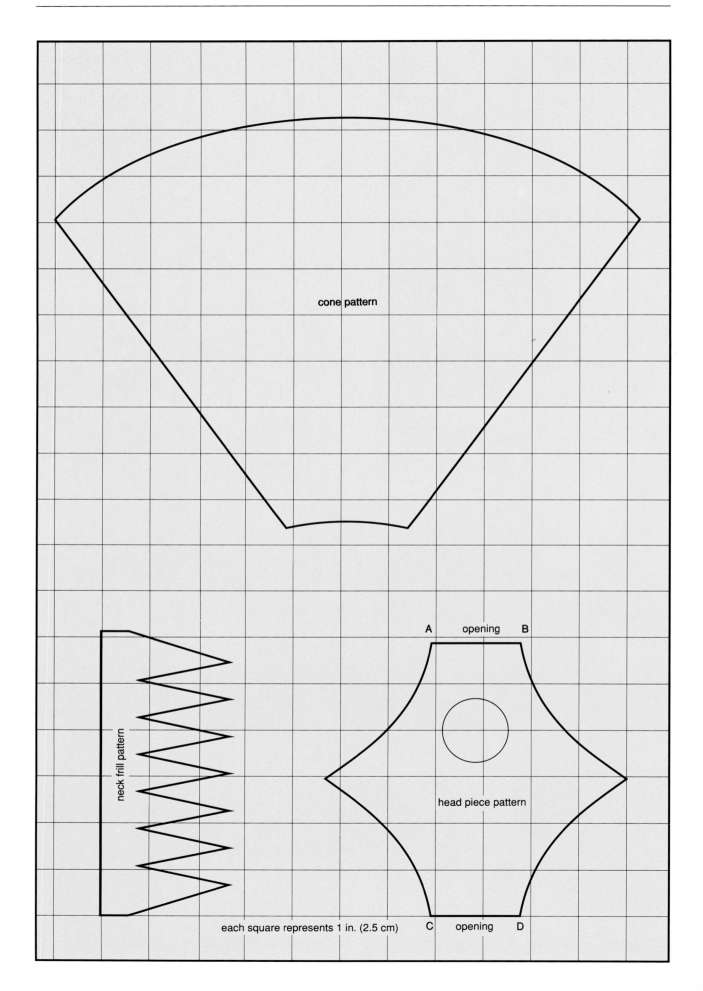

cone pattern

neck frill pattern

A   opening   B

head piece pattern

each square represents 1 in. (2.5 cm)   C   opening   D

Heirloom Dressed Baby Doll

scissors, pins
tape measure
1²⁄₃ yd (1.5 m) of 44 in. (112 cm)
wide white cotton lawn
2¹⁄₃ yd (2.1 m) of 2³⁄₈ in. (6 cm) wide
Swiss embroidered lace edging
No. 80 cotton thread
iron
white embroidery floss
No. 10 crewel embroidery needle
12½ in. (32 cm) of 1 in. (2.5 cm) wide
Swiss embroidered lace insertion
2¾ yd (2.5 m) of ¹⁄₁₆ in. (2 mm) wide satin ribbon
1½ yd (1.4 m) of ³⁄₈ in. (10 mm) wide
French cotton lace edging
19¾ in. (50 cm) of ⅛ in. (3 mm) wide entredeux
1 snap fastener
6 in. (15 cm) iron-on interfacing
29½ in. (75 cm) of ³⁄₈ in. (10 mm) wide
double-sided satin ribbon

Embroidery stitches used:
double feather stitch

This heirloom outfit has been hand sewn, but you can, of course, make the gown and bonnet using a sewing machine.

Enlarge the scaled patterns as instructed (page 4) and leave aside until needed. Note that stitching lines have been marked, representing a ³⁄₈ in. (10 mm) seam allowance.

Skirt

Cut one 32¾ in. (83 cm) length of the lawn fabric for the skirt.

Pull a thread ½ in. (1 cm) in from each selvage and cut along the pulled-thread lines. Cut 43¼ in. (1.1 m) of the 2³⁄₈ in. (6 cm) wide Swiss lace edging and attach to one long edge of the fabric with a fine French seam. This will be the bottom of the skirt.

To prepare the pin tucks, measure ³⁄₁₆ in. (5 mm) up from the seam joining the lace to the skirt and pull a thread the entire width of the skirt. Pull five more threads each ½ in. (13 mm) apart.

From the sixth pulled thread, measure upward ⅞ in. (22 mm) and pull another set of six threads ½ in. (13 mm) apart.

Repeat the above step to make another six pulled threads. There should be three lots of six rows of pulled threads.

Fold wrong side together along the first pulled thread, press with an iron and evenly stitch ⅛ in. (3 mm) from the edge. Repeat with the remaining 17 pulled threads. Press the tucks toward the hemline.

Measure ⅜ in. (10 mm) up from the last pin tuck and work a row of double feather stitch with one strand of white embroidery floss. Join the back seam together with a fine French seam, leaving a ⅝ in. (16 mm) opening at the top. Roll and whip the raw edge of this opening. Stitch a row of gathering stitches along the top of the skirt as shown in diagram 1.

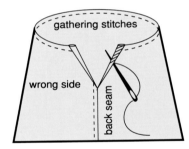

Diagram 1

Bodice

Prepare the center yoke by cutting a piece of fabric 5½ x 8 in. (14 x 20 cm) on the straight of the grain. Measure 1⅝ in. (4 cm) down from one of the short sides and pull a thread for first pin tuck. Pull two more threads ½ in. (13 mm) apart. Measure down 1 in. (2.5 cm) from third pulled thread and draw another thread. Pull another two threads ½ in. (13 mm) apart. Measure down 1 in. (2.5 cm) from the sixth pulled thread and pull another three threads ½ in. (13 mm) apart (as in diagram 2).

Fold along the first pulled thread, press and stitch ⅛ in. (3 mm) from the folded edge to make a pin tuck. Make eight more pin tucks along the pulled threads. Press the tucks toward the bottom. Position the

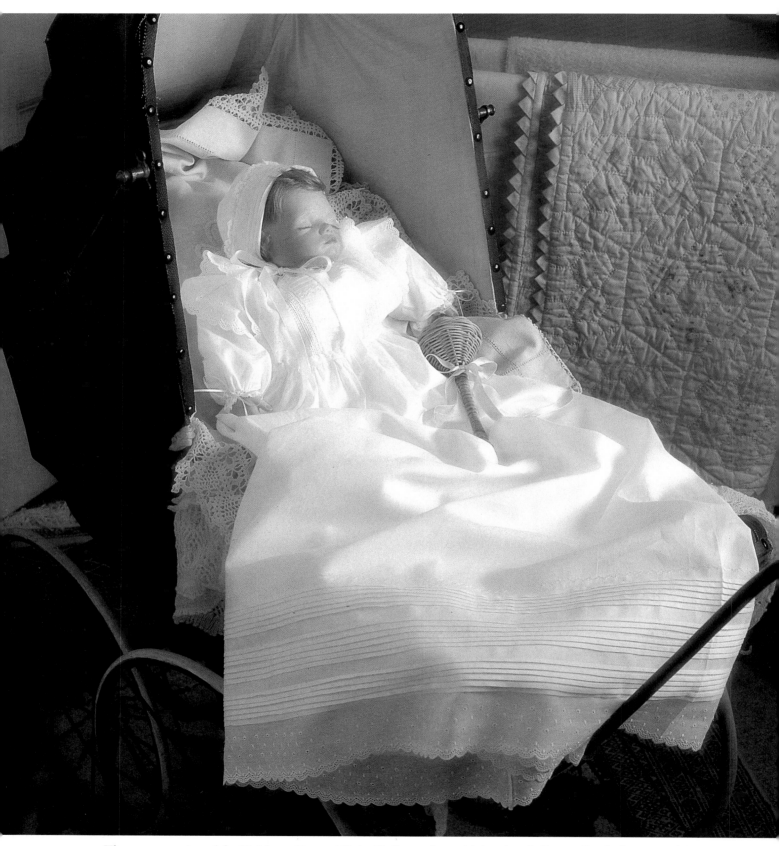

The serene setting of the Heirloom Dressed Baby Doll complete with handmade Rattan Rattle (see page 52).

center yoke pattern with the bottom of the pattern level with the bottom of the pin-tucked fabric piece. Pin to the fabric and cut out (as in diagram 3).

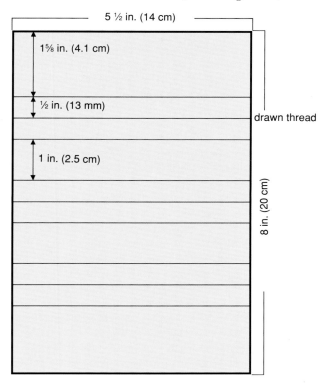

Diagram 2

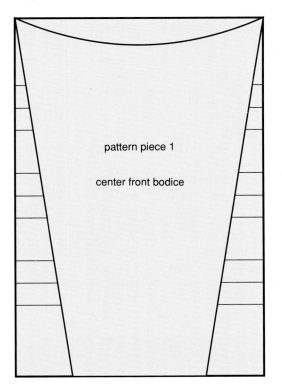

Diagram 3

Cut out another piece of the fabric with the center yoke pattern and pin to the back of the pin-tucked piece (two thicknesses of fabric). Cut the Swiss embroidered insertion lace in half, and with the right sides together, place along each side of the center yoke panel. Stitch along the seam line as shown in diagram 4.

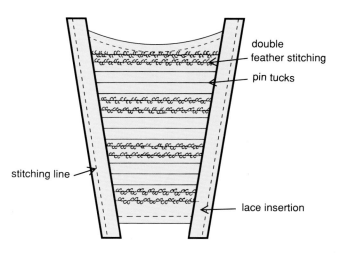

Diagram 4

Trim the seams to $\frac{1}{16}$ in. (2 mm) and whip or buttonhole stitch to avoid fraying. Press. On the right side of the front panel, stitch two rows of double feather stitch in each gap between the groups of pin tucks and two more rows above and two rows below the pin tucks (diagram 4). Finish with a row of double feather stitch close to the seam line on the insertion lace.

Cut out the back and side panels from the lawns, following pattern pieces Nos. 2 and 3. Join the shoulder seams with a fine French seam. Turn under $\frac{3}{4}$ in. (19 mm) of the center back toward the fold line. Fold again on the fold line and blind stitch into place. Cut two strips of Swiss embroidered lace edging $15\frac{3}{4}$ in. (40 cm) long.

Lay the back and side panels flat. Place the wrong side of the lace to the right side of the side panel along the edge and up to the mark at the neckline. Roll and whip the lace edge at the back opening and place the wrong side of the lace along the back neck edge to the mark. Gather the remaining lace to fit between the marks. Tack into place. Repeat with the other side and back panel (diagram 5).

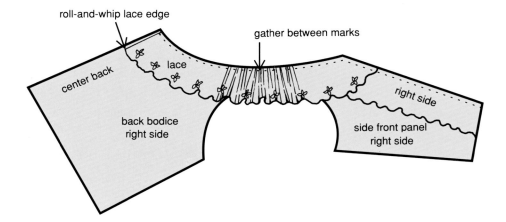

roll-and-whip lace edge

gather between marks

center back

lace

right side

back bodice
right side

side front panel
right side

Diagram 5

Attach to the center yoke panel by placing the Swiss embroidered insertion lace, right sides together, over the lace edging and stitching along the stitching line. Repeat with the other side (see diagram 6).

Cut 18½ in. (47 cm) of the French cotton lace edging. Fold over each cut end ³⁄₁₆ in. (5 mm) and buttonhole stitch. Whip stitch to the top of the neck bias (as in diagram 7), gathering gently as you stitch.

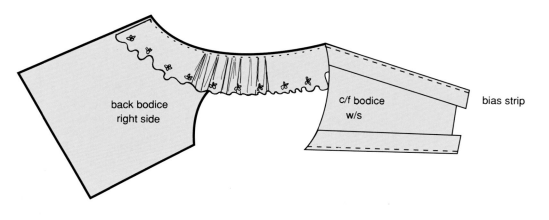

back bodice
right side

c/f bodice
w/s

bias strip

Diagram 6

Trim the seam to ¹⁄₁₆ in. (2 mm) and whip or buttonhole stitch to avoid fraying. Press toward the center of the insertion lace. On the right side, stitch a row of double feather stitch along the seam line to match the other side of the insertion. Cut a bias strip of lawn 18½ x 1⅝ in. (47 x 4 cm), fold in half lengthwise and press, to iron out the stretch. With the right sides together, place the binding around the neckline, raw edges together and stitch into place. Sew the seam ⅝ in. (16 mm) from the raw edge. Press. On the right side of the bodice, embroider a row of double feather stitching onto the front of the bias strip. Turn the folded edge of the bias over to the back and blind stitch close to the seam. Leave the ends open to insert a ¹⁄₁₆ in. (2 mm) ribbon.

Sleeves

Roll and whip the bottom edge of the sleeve and attach the entredeux. Whip the French cotton lace edging to the other edge of the entredeux. Sew the sleeve sides with a fine French seam. Using pattern piece No. 5 as a guide, cut two lengths of Swiss embroidered lace edging for the head of the sleeve. Stitch up the side seams with a fine French seam. Place the wrong side of the lace to the right side of the sleeve and tack together around the head (see diagram 8).

Sew a row of gathering stitches between the marks on pattern piece No. 4. Stitch the sleeves into the armholes, gathering the sleeve head to fit. Trim the

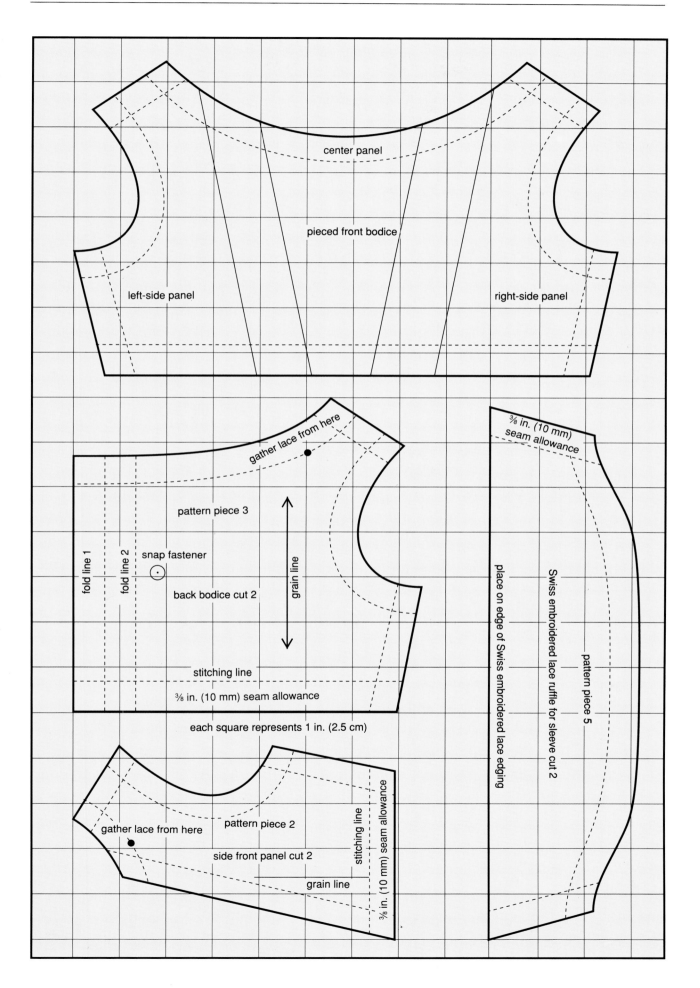

center panel

pieced front bodice

left-side panel

right-side panel

gather lace from here

pattern piece 3

fold line 1

fold line 2

snap fastener

back bodice cut 2

grain line

stitching line

⅜ in. (10 mm) seam allowance

each square represents 1 in. (2.5 cm)

gather lace from here

pattern piece 2

side front panel cut 2

stitching line

grain line

⅜ in. (10 mm) seam allowance

⅜ in. (10 mm) seam allowance

place on edge of Swiss embroidered lace edging

Swiss embroidered lace ruffle for sleeve cut 2

pattern piece 5

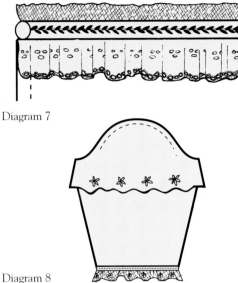

Diagram 7

Diagram 8

seam to 1/16 in. (2 mm) and whip or fine-buttonhole stitch the raw edges to avoid fraying.

Attaching the Bodice to the Skirt

Cut a casing for the ribbon at the waist 1⅛ in. (2.8 cm) wide and ¾ in. (19 mm) longer than the edge of the bodice. Turn under ⅜ in. (10 mm) along each edge. Place the casing wrong side to right side along the waist edge of the bodice and tack into place.

Pull the gathering around the skirt waist and spread evenly to fit the bodice. Place right side to right side; stitch along the seam line. Trim the seam to 1/16 in. (2 mm) and whip or buttonhole stitch the raw edges to avoid fraying. Press. Fold under a ⅜ in. (10 mm) turning on the casing. Press up toward the neckline. Work double feather stitching along the casing before blind stitching it onto the bodice. Leave the ends open to thread the ribbon through.

Thread the 1/16 in. (2 mm) ribbon through the neckline, waist and sleeves. Sew a snap fastener at the back bodice opening.

Bonnet

Cut a piece of the fabric 8 x 11 in. (20 x 28 cm) along the straight of the grain. Pull a thread to be sure the cut edge is straight. Measure 1⅜ in. (3.5 cm) from the straight edge and pull a thread to make the first pin tuck. Pull two more threads ⅞ in. (22 mm) apart. Press along the line of the first pulled thread and

stitch a pin tuck ⅛ in. (3 mm) from the fold. Make two more pin tucks in the same way. Press the tucks away from the cut edge.

Press the iron-on interfacing to the wrong side of the pin-tucked fabric; then place the straight edge of bonnet pattern piece No. 6 along the straight edge of the interfaced pin-tucked fabric and cut out the bonnet shape. Cut another piece of fabric the same shape for the lining (see diagram 9).

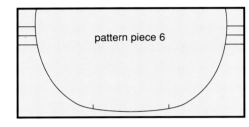

pattern piece 6

Diagram 9

Measure ⅝ in. (16 mm) from the straight edge of the pin-tucked fabric and work a row of double feather stitch with white embroidery thread. Cut 20½ in. (52 cm) of the French cotton lace edging and pull a gathering thread on the header; space gathers evenly along the stitching line between the markers. Tack into place. With the right sides together, stitch the lining to the pin-tucked piece along the stitching line between the marks. Trim the seam and turn right side out and press.

Cut the crown section of the bonnet twice from pattern piece No. 7. Interface one of the pieces, then place the two pieces together, right side to right side, and stitch along the lower edge. Trim the seam. Turn to the right side and press.

Sew a gathering thread (through all thicknesses) between the marks on the bonnet top. Then, with the pin-tucked side of the bonnet underneath, stitch only the interfaced section of the crown to the bonnet top, pulling the top's gathering stitches to fit between the marks on the crown. Trim the seam and press toward the crown. Turn under the seam allowance on the crown lining and blind stitch along the seam line. Press.

Turn the bonnet so that the pin tucks are on the underside. Fold back 1⅛ in. (2.9 cm) of the bonnet edge to show the pin tucks, embroidery and lace edging. Press into place. Cut the wide double-sided satin ribbon in half and attach to the folded corner of the bonnet for ties.

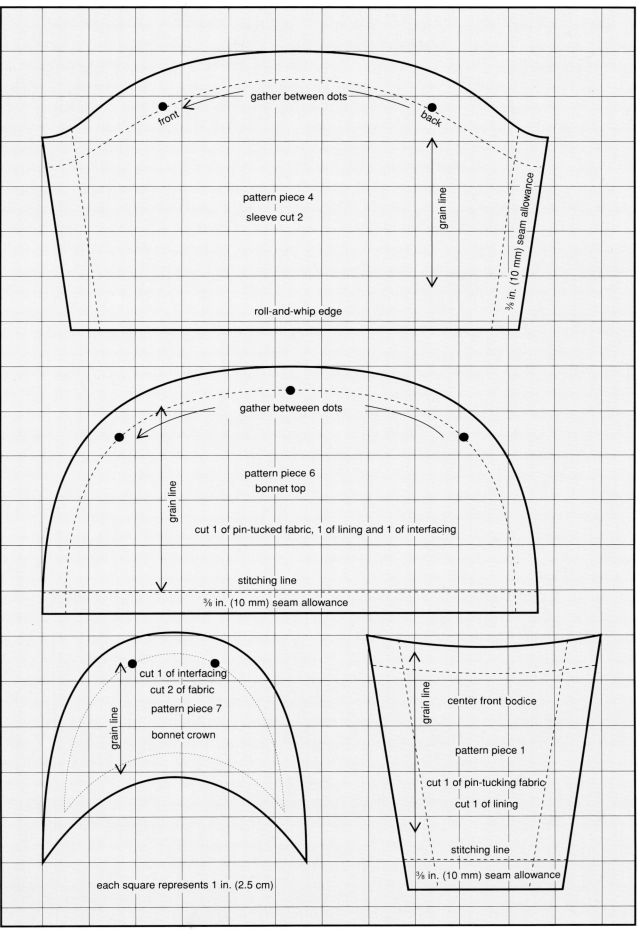

gather between dots

front   back

grain line

pattern piece 4

sleeve cut 2

⅜ in. (10 mm) seam allowance

roll-and-whip edge

gather betweeen dots

grain line

pattern piece 6
bonnet top

cut 1 of pin-tucked fabric, 1 of lining and 1 of interfacing

stitching line

⅜ in. (10 mm) seam allowance

cut 1 of interfacing

cut 2 of fabric

pattern piece 7

bonnet crown

grain line

grain line

center front bodice

pattern piece 1

cut 1 of pin-tucking fabric

cut 1 of lining

stitching line

⅜ in. (10 mm) seam allowance

each square represents 1 in. (2.5 cm)

Rattan Rattle

*4 stakes of No. 3 round basketry reed
16 in. (40 cm) long
bucket of water
½ oz (15 g) of No. 1 or No. 2 round reed
for weaving
rubber bands
⅜ in. (10 mm) jingle bell
scissors
quick-drying craft glue
flat oval reed (like that used for chair-seat caning) or
binder cane (which still wears its shiny rattan skin)
fine sandpaper
19¾ in. (50 cm) of ⅝ in. (15 mm) wide ribbon*

To prepare the reed for weaving, soak in a bucket of water until it is flexible (approximately 1 hour). Thin reed will dry out fast, making it difficult to manipulate. Plunge it into warm water to re-soften quickly, so that you can keep working.

Make a cross with the four stakes as shown in diagram 1.

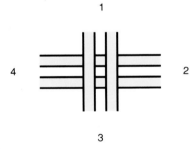

Diagram 1

Use the No. 1 or No. 2 round reed to weave through the four heavier stakes. To begin weaving, take the reed over 1, under 2, over 3, under 4, crossing the reed between stakes (as in diagram 2).

This is termed pairing. Continue for two rows.

Diagram 2

After the first two rows, separate the stakes to singles and continue pairing, pressing the weaving

and the stakes away from you. Keep contouring the stakes to maintain a dome shape. Weave nine rounds.

Pull the stakes together at the bottom and wrap a rubber band around them. Add a third piece of round weaving reed and wale for two rounds (refer to diagram 3). To wale is to weave over two stakes, under one, over two, under one, alternating the one that is woven under.

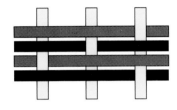

Diagram 3

Insert the bell. Trim off the third piece of weaving reed and continue to pair, following the shape of the stakes as they come in for approximately nine rounds. Fold the weaving reed to the inside and trim with the scissors to neaten. Secure the stakes in a neat round stem, being sure that none cross over each other and hold with adequate rubber bands. Cut off the ends of the stakes 4¾ in. (12 cm) from the last row of pairing.

Make a loop approximately ⅜ in. (10 mm) in diameter using two weaving reed pieces twisted together, and glue it onto the end of the handle as shown in diagram 4. Run glue along the handle to hold the stakes; allow to dry. Wrap the oval reed (chair-seating cane) or binder cane around the handle from the top to the bottom, butting the edge on each wrap. To finish off, thread the cane back under itself.

Sand the handle lightly. Weave the ribbon through the stakes at the base of the dome and tie in a bow. (See picture on page 46.)

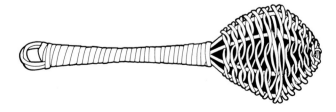

Diagram 4

Embroidered Teddy Bear

Finished size 15¾ in. (40 cm) tall

*29½ in. (75 cm) washed muslin
scissors, pins
6 in. (15 cm) each of 6 or 8 co-ordinating fabrics
(choose from silk, satin, velvet and cotton)
iron
variety of ribbons, laces, embroidery threads, beads
and other interesting embellishments
sewing machine
piece of felt approximately 12 in. square (30.5 cm sq.)
1 bag of toy filling or stuffing
4 sets of bear joints, if available
1 pair of ⅝ in. (15 mm) bear eyes
black or brown embroidery floss, appropriate needle
27½ in. (70 cm) of 1 in. (2.5 cm) wide double-sided
satin ribbon*

Embroidery stitches used:
    herringbone stitch
    chevron stitch
    blind stitch
    feather stitch
    satin stitch

Enlarge the scaled patterns carefully following the instructions on page 4 and being sure to transfer all information shown on the patterns. A ¼ in. (6 mm) seam allowance is included on each piece.

Using the muslin, cut out each piece of the bear except the paw pads, marking the wrong side of the fabric with the relevant information from the pattern piece. Where two pieces are to be cut, be sure to reverse one of the pattern pieces so that you will have a right and left side for the bear.

Cover each piece with crazy patchwork. Detailed instructions for piecing the crazy patchwork can be found on page 147, (Christmas Stocking and Tree Skirt). When all piecing is completed, press each piece carefully on the wrong side. Hide the seams of the patchwork with old fashioned embroidery stitches such as herringbone, chevron and feather stitches and plain and gathered laces, beads and ribbons. Antique buttons and other small treasures are also excellent embellishments.

After completing the beading and embroidery, trim the edges of each piece even with the foundation muslin fabric.

The two foot pads and two paw pads can be made as a special feature of your bear. You could include the name of the recipient of the bear and other little messages. The pads could be made from velvet, satin or cream flannel and left plain; or you might like to use evenweave embroidery cloth such as Aida and work a small cross stitch design on it. These ideas make your bear very personal and individual. Decide on the fabric and cut the paw pads out following the pattern pieces.

Sew the center front seam and the center back seam, leaving space open in the back for stuffing. Stitch the side seams from the neck down to the bottom and up the other side in one operation (see diagram 1).

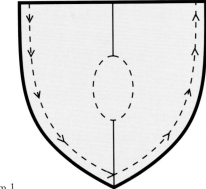

Diagram 1

Sew the paw pads to the inner arm pieces. Sew the outer and inner arms together, easing the top of the outer arm to fit the inner arm and leaving space to stuff (diagram 2).

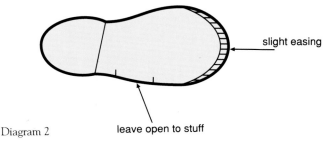
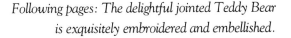

slight easing

Diagram 2   leave open to stuff

*Following pages: The delightful jointed Teddy Bear
is exquisitely embroidered and embellished.*

THE STRANGE BOY

Sew an inner and an outer leg together, leaving the bottom open and a space on the side for stuffing. Pin and baste the paw pads in the opening at the bottom of the leg. Stitch around carefully. Repeat for the other leg.

Sew the two side head pieces together from the chin to the neck. Sew the darts where marked. Pin the head center piece into position, matching the center of the nose with the chin seam and the bottom of the head center level with the neck edge of the side head pieces, easing to fit smoothly. Carefully stitch in place as shown in diagram 3.

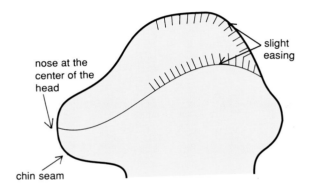

Diagram 3

Clip any loose threads, clip seam allowance where necessary and turn all pieces to the right side.

Attach the arms and the legs with teddy bear joints. If these are not available you could use buttons or sew the arms and legs onto the body. Using the pattern piece marked felt only, cut out eight pieces of felt and make a hole in the center of each. Make a small hole in the inner arm and the upper body at the point marked for joint placement. Place a piece of felt on one joint disk, push through the hole in the arm and then through the body hole. On the inside of the body, on the disk post place a piece of felt, then the joint washer and finally the lock washer. Push right down until firm. Repeat for the other arm and the two legs.

Firmly stuff each arm and leg. Be sure to pack the filling tight for the best result, pushing well into the area around the joints and along the seams to give the bear nicely rounded arms and legs. Hand sew the openings closed using a blind stitch. Make a small hole in the places marked for the eyes. Insert the eyes

and secure with the washer locks. Firmly stuff the body, once more pushing stuffing well into the joints and into the corners and seams. Stitch the opening closed. Add more stuffing through the top until overfull. This will blend with the head stuffing when the head is stitched on. Stuff the head until round and firm, paying particular attention to the nose area and the seams. Turn the seam allowance in on the neck edge and baste.

Line up the body front with the chin seam, the side seams with the dart seams, and the center back seams with the center of the head piece. Pin in place. Carefully blind stitch the head to the body.

Using either a dark brown or black embroidery thread, embroider the nose and mouth. Use diagram 4 as a guide.

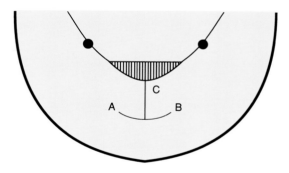

Diagram 4

Satin stitch the nose with a long thread. With the same thread, bring the needle out at point A, in again at B, out at C, then loop the thread over A/B thread and pull up to form a slight curve for the mouth. Finish the thread in the nose stitches as invisibly as possible and then snip off.

Sew two ear pieces together and turn right side out, repeat for the other ear, turn in the seam allowance and baste. They can be left as is or very, very lightly stuffed. Stitch the bottom edges together and remove the basting. Position on the head using the ear line mark as a guide. Blind stitch in place at the back of the ear, so that they angle slightly towards the front.

Finish the teddy bear by tying a ribbon bow around his neck.

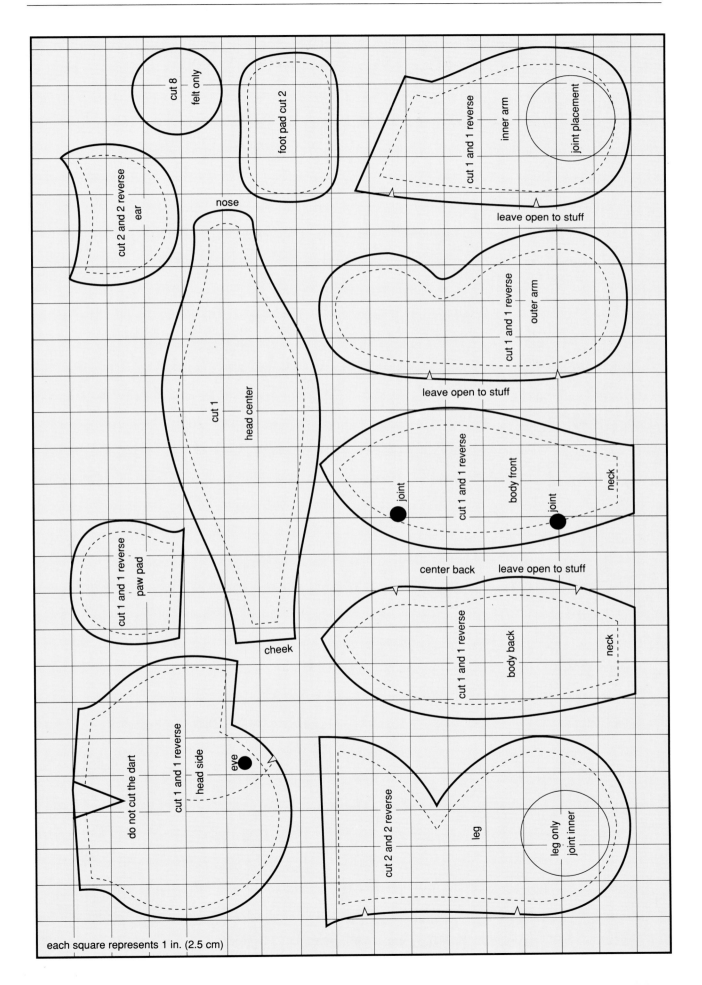

cut 8
felt only

foot pad cut 2

cut 1 and 1 reverse
inner arm

joint placement

leave open to stuff

cut 2 and 2 reverse
ear

nose

cut 1 and 1 reverse
outer arm

leave open to stuff

cut 1
head center

cut 1 and 1 reverse
paw pad

joint

cut 1 and 1 reverse
body front

joint

neck

cheek

center back   leave open to stuff

cut 1 and 1 reverse
body back

neck

do not cut the dart

cut 1 and 1 reverse
head side

eye

cut 2 and 2 reverse

leg

leg only
joint inner

each square represents 1 in. (2.5 cm)

CHAPTER 2

Lady's Boudoir

THE VICTORIAN woman was far more liberated than women of previous eras. It was considered acceptable for her to bathe in the sea, play tennis and even hike. A Victorian lady was always seen wearing lace at her throat and wrists, clean boots, spotless gloves and a clean, crisp white handkerchief.

The Victorian woman believed that a love of beauty was a natural human characteristic and that her role was to look as beautiful as she could. Being well dressed was very important and an expression of the Victorian woman's personality.

Her boudoir (from the French for "a place to pout") was her own exclusive place, where she could gather her tokens and keepsakes around her. The boudoir revealed her love of beauty and the importance placed on personal grooming.

Above: Detail from a Victorian shawl.
Opposite: The Victorian woman's boudoir was a place of tranquillity where she could surround herself with beautiful objects.

Heirloom Nightgown

To fit bust 32–34 in. (81–86 cm) waist 24–28 in. (66–71 cm)

3¾ yd (3.5 m) of 45 in. (115 cm)
wide white cotton voile
scissors, tape measure
2 yd (1.8 m) of ¾ in. (19 mm) wide Swiss
embroidered beading
3¾ yd (3.5 m) of ½ in. (13 mm)
wide white
French insertion lace

sewing machine
cotton sewing thread size 90, quilting thread
No. 10 crewel embroidery needle, pins
iron
1¾ yd (1.5 m) of ⅛ in. (3 mm) wide double-sided
satin ribbon
33½ in. (85 cm) of ⅝ in. (15 mm) wide Swiss
lace edging
1½ yd (1.4 m) of ⅛ in. (3 mm) entredeux
2⅝ yd (2.5 m) of ⅜ in. (10 mm) Swiss
entredeux beading
2½ yd (2.3 m) of 1½ in. (3.8 cm) wide white
French lace edging
18 in. (46 cm) of ⅝ in. (16 mm) wide white
French lace edging
11 pearl buttons, ³⁄₁₆ in. (5 mm)
2¼ yd (2.1 m) of ³⁄₁₆ in. (5 mm) wide double-sided
satin ribbon

For ease of stitching use natural fiber fabrics.

Enlarge the scaled patterns as instructed on page 4. Straighten one edge of the fabric: make a tiny clip in the selvage edge of the fabric, pick up a single crosswise thread and gently pull. If the thread breaks, cut along the pulled-thread line until you reach the break, then pick up the thread again. If you need a vertical strip of fabric, or if removing the selvage, use the same method with lengthwise threads.

Measure along the selvage 16 in. (41 cm) and pull another thread. Cut along this line. Next remove both the selvages from the piece of fabric, using the method described to ensure straight cuts (refer to diagram 1).

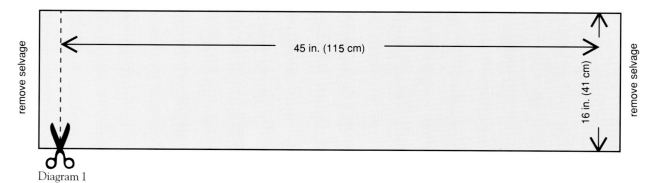

Diagram 1

The fine detail of the bodice of the Heirloom Nightgown has a look of elegance and romanticism.

From this piece of fabric cut:
1 strip 2⅝ in. x 16 in. (6.7 x 41 cm) left front
1 strip 1¾ x 16 in. (4.4 x 41 cm) right front
2 strips 3⅝ x 16 in. (9.2 x 41 cm) pin-tucked panel
2 strips 2 x 16 in. (5 x 41 cm) front plackets
2 strips 2¾ x 16 in. (7 x 41 cm) underarm sides

Cut the ¾ in. (19 mm wide) Swiss embroidered beading into four pieces, each 16 in. (41 cm) long.

Cut the ½ in. (13 mm) wide French lace insertion into eight pieces, each 16 in. (41 cm) long.

Attach a piece of the French lace to either side of each piece of the beading; with right sides together and using a small straight stitch, "stitch in the ditch" of the beading.

Make sure the stitching line is along the reinforced edge of the French lace. Trim away the excess fabric from the beading to measure ⅛ in. (3 mm), then roll-and-whip both edges of each piece. Turn right side out and press carefully. You should now have four strips of pieced lace resembling diagram 2.

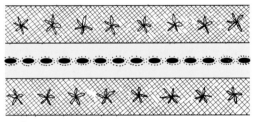

Diagram 2

To make pin tucks, use the folded-fabric method: pull a thread for each tuck; fold the fabric on each of the pulled threads, and machine-sew to the desired width from the folded edge using a single needle on a standard presser foot.

The strip of fabric that measures 2⅝ x 16 in. (6.7 x 41 cm) needs three very small pin tucks in the middle of the fabric. Do the center pin tuck first, then the ones either side, spacing them ³⁄₁₆ in. (5 mm) apart. Repeat on the piece of fabric that measures 1¾ x 16 in. (4.4 x 41 cm).

Note: The pin tucks are worked along the longest dimension of the fabric.

On the two strips of fabric measuring 3⅝ x 16 in. (9.2 x 41 cm), find the middle of the strip and make a small pin tuck, then stitch two pin tucks either side of the center, spacing them ⅜ in. (10 mm) apart.

Once the pin-tucked pieces have been completed, sew the lace strips and the pin-tucked pieces together, referring to diagram 3: with right sides together, straight stitch along the reinforced edge of the lace leaving a seam allowance of ³⁄₁₆ in. (5 mm); then roll-and-whip the edge of the fabric. Attach a narrow strip of pin tucking to a lace strip, then the larger pin-tucked strip to the other side of the lace strip. Next attach a second piece of lace to the other side of the large pin-tucked strip; lastly attach a strip of fabric measuring 2¾ x 16 in. (7 x 41 cm) to the other edge of the last lace strip. Repeat this process to make two identical pieces.

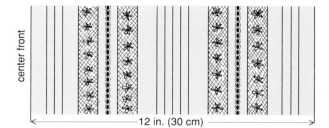

center front

──────────12 in. (30 cm)──────────

Diagram 3

Each piece should measure at least 12 in. (30 cm) and be 16 in. (41 cm) deep (as in diagram 3). Thread the ⅛ in. (3 mm) wide double-sided satin ribbon through the beading.

Lay the front yoke pattern piece over each of the pieced panels. When cutting each side, be sure to lay the pattern identically on each piece, as it looks better if the two sides are even. Lay the back bodice pattern over the remaining fabric and cut out.

Next, cut a length of the Swiss embroidered lace edging to match the left front yoke and attach it ⅝ in. (16 mm) from the center front (diagram 4): lay the lace edging right side to right side, with the scalloped edge facing away from the center front. Stitch in place and trim the excess fabric from the lace, then turn the lace, so the scalloped edge is now level with the center front line (diagram 5). Gently press.

To attach the plackets to the front openings, stitch one of the 2 x 16 in. (5 x 41 cm) pieces, right sides together, to the front edge opening of each of the left and the right fronts. Be careful not to catch the scalloped edge of the front left yoke. Join the front yokes to the back bodice at the shoulder; the seam allowance is ⅜ in. (10 mm). Trim the seam allowance in half—to ³⁄₁₆ in. (5 mm)—and with a small zigzag, roll-and-whip the trimmed edge. Sew the side seams in the same way. Turn the placket strip to the wrong side along the stitched line and press; fold the strip in half lengthwise again and press again. Repeat for the other front side. This gives a neat edge-to-edge front closing.

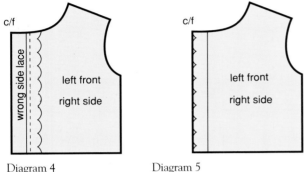

Diagram 4   Diagram 5

Cut another length of the Swiss embroidered edging ¾ in. (19 mm) longer than the total length of the neck edge and a piece of the ⅛ in. (3 mm) wide entredeux the same length.

Join the lace edging to the entredeux by laying the right sides together and stitching in the ditch; trim the excess fabric, then roll-and-whip the edges together. Open out and carefully press flat. With the right side of the bodice facing, lay the entredeux around the neck edge—there should be an excess of ¾ in. (19 mm) at the front neck edge of each side.

Straight stitch in place, trim the excess seam allowance and press open. Turn back the excess at the front neck edge and hand stitch in place to neaten.

Cut two lengths of Swiss entredeux beading the same length as the bottom edge of the bodice and apply by stitching in the ditch of the entredeux. Trim the excess fabric on the entredeux and zigzag stitch over the seam allowance.

Cut two lengths of cotton voile for the skirt 45 in. (115 cm), by the width, by measuring 45 in. (115 cm) along the selvage, pulling a thread and cutting along the pulled thread line; repeat for the second length.

Join the sides of the skirt with French seams.

Roll-and-whip the top edge of the skirt. With your machine's stitch length set to maximum to gather, use the quilting thread and straight stitch ⅛ in. (3 mm) in from the raw edge. Then set to zigzag, so that the stitching clears the machine gathering—do

not catch the gathering thread with the needle. Pull the gathering thread and distribute the gathers evenly.

Make a rolled hem on the bottom edge of the skirt and attach the 1½ in. (3.8 cm) French lace edging (diagram 6) to cover the bottom edge of the skirt.

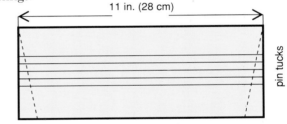

Diagram 6

Position three ⅜ in. (10 mm) wide finished tucks above the hemline, the first ¾ in. (19 mm) above the hem, the others ⅝ in. (16 mm) apart. Pin the skirt to the entredeux edging the bodice, with the skirt seams aligned to the side seams of the bodice, right sides together. Stitch in the ditch of the entredeux. Trim the excess fabric from the entredeux and zig-zag stitch over the seam allowance.

To make the sleeves, start with the cuffs: cut two squares of fabric 6 x 11 in. (15 x 28 cm).

As previously described, place five pin tucks ⅜ in. (10 mm) apart across the middle of each of these two pieces of fabric. Place the cuff pattern piece over the pin-tucked piece of fabric and cut out two cuffs (see diagram 7). Use the same pattern to cut out two cuff linings.

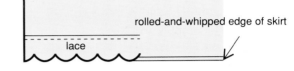

Diagram 7

Cut a 9 in. (23 cm) length of the ⅝ in. (16 mm) wide French lace edging. Place the right side of the lace along the narrow edge of the right side of the cuff; place the cuff lining on top, sandwiching the lace inside. Stitch on three sides as shown in diagram 8.

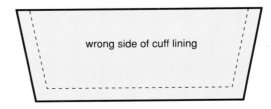

Diagram 8

Turn the cuff and lining right side out and press gently. The lace edging will now be on the bottom edge of the cuff as shown in diagram 9.

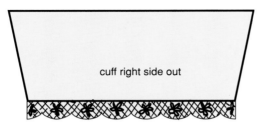

cuff right side out

Diagram 9

Cut the two sleeve plackets from the pattern piece and roll-and-whip on the long edge of each piece. Pin the placket to the clipped edge of the sleeve. With the right side of the sleeve facing you, straight stitch along the seam line almost to the clip point indicated with an A in diagram 10. The seam allowance is $\frac{3}{16}$ in. (5 mm). Stitch slowly to the clip point, hand cranking the last few stitches. Leaving the needle in the fabric, lift the presser foot and rearrange the fabric to make sure no puckers form and lower the presser foot. Hand crank the first few stitches past the clip point, then stitch the remainder of the seam—refer to diagram 10.

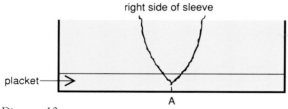

right side of sleeve

placket

A

Diagram 10

Trim the seam allowance. Fold the placket in half, back into its natural position. Turn right sides in and stitch at an angle across the top of the placket to help it sit correctly (diagram 11).

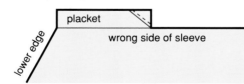

placket

lower edge

wrong side of sleeve

Diagram 11

Close the underarm seam of the sleeve with a French seam. Gather the bottom of the sleeve to fit the cuff. Pin the cuff to the sleeve right sides together, matching all the notched markings. The cuff ends should be flush with both edges of the placket. Pull the gathering threads to ease in the fullness of the sleeve and distribute evenly. Stitch in place (diagram 12).

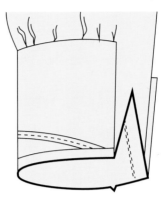

Diagram 12

Fold the cuff down and press the seam toward the cuff. Bring the folded edge of the cuff facing to the stitching line on the wrong side of the sleeve and slip stitch in place (as in diagram 13). Remove any visible gathering threads.

Diagram 13

Run two rows of gathering threads between the notches at the top of the sleeve, the first row $\frac{1}{8}$ in. (3 mm) from the raw edge. Pull up the gathering threads to fit the armhole, concentrating the gathers at the top of the sleeve. Straight stitch in place with a $\frac{3}{16}$ in. (5 mm) seam allowance. Trim and zigzag stitch for a neat finish.

Work three buttonhole loops of thread on each cuff, one each at the top and the bottom and one in the middle. Sew on the buttons. Work five evenly spaced thread buttonhole loops down the front of the bodice; sew on the buttons. Thread two rows of the $\frac{3}{16}$ in. (5 mm) ribbon through the entredeux beading at the waist. Press to finish.

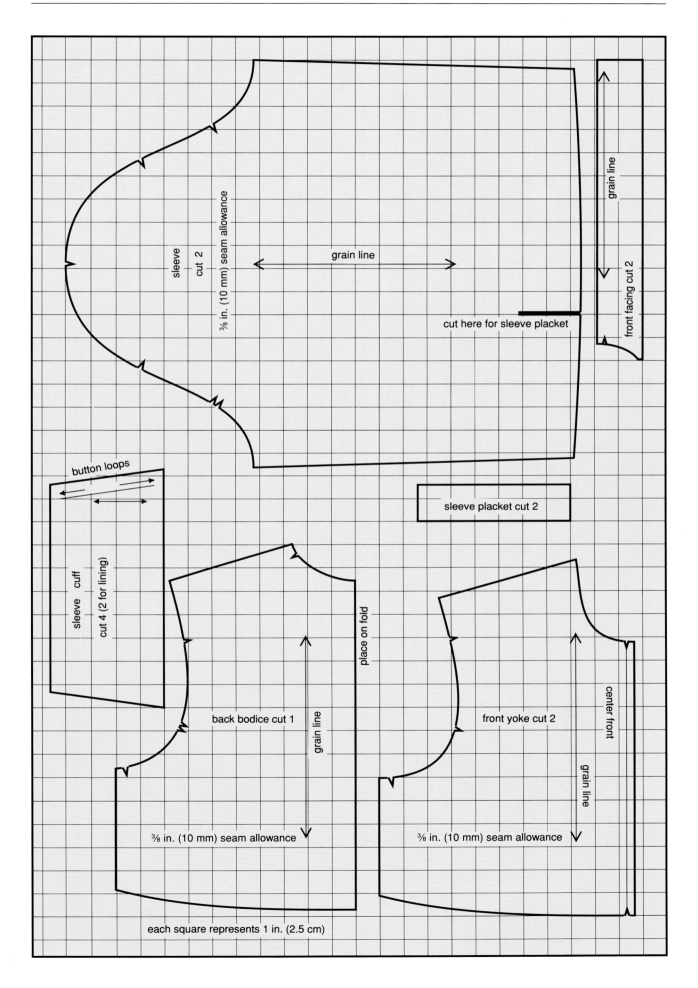

sleeve
cut 2

⅜ in. (10 mm) seam allowance

grain line

cut here for sleeve placket

grain line

front facing cut 2

button loops

sleeve placket cut 2

sleeve cuff

cut 4 (2 for lining)

place on fold

back bodice cut 1

grain line

front yoke cut 2

center front

grain line

⅜ in. (10 mm) seam allowance

⅜ in. (10 mm) seam allowance

each square represents 1 in. (2.5 cm)

Victorian Sewing Bag

thin cardboard
pin, string, pencil, scissors
24 in. (61 cm) print fabric
24 in. (61 cm) plain fabric to co-ordinate
sheet of thin plastic
iron
needle and thread, seam ripper
sewing machine
1¾ yd (1.6 m) cotton beading lace
4⅓ yd (4 m) of ⅛ in. (3 mm) wide double-sided
satin ribbon

2⅜ yd (2.2 m) of ⅜ in. (10 mm) cotton edging lace
1¾ yd (1.6 m) of 1⅛ in. (3 cm) wide gathered cotton
edging with a beading header
3¼ yd (3 m) of cord
2 wooden beads

To make the pattern pieces for the Victorian Sewing Bag, begin with circles: push a pin into the cardboard, tie a piece of string around it, tie a pencil to the other end, and holding the string taut, draw a circle (diagram 1).

Victorian Sewing Bag (center), lace-making (left) and antique Spanish chatelaine circa 1836 (right).

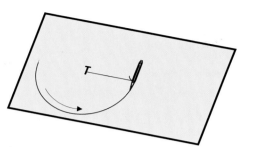

Diagram 1

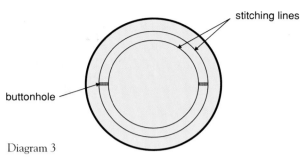

stitching lines

buttonhole

Diagram 3

You need three circles. One has a diameter of 19¾ in. (50 cm)—which means the string will be half that length, or 9⅞ in. (25 cm) long—one has a diameter of 16½ in. (42 cm) and the third, a diameter of 5⅞ in. (15 cm). Cut out the pattern pieces.

Use the pattern pieces to cut out one large circle each of the print fabric and the plain fabric; one medium circle of each and one small circle of the plastic sheeting only.

Fold the large print fabric circle in half and press lightly. Make two ⅜ in. (10 mm) buttonholes 1¼ in. (3.2 cm) from the outside edge of the circle, on the fold line. Slit the buttonholes carefully with the seam ripper (see diagram 2).

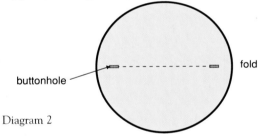

buttonhole

fold

Diagram 2

Join the large print circle and the large plain circle with a ¼ in. (6 mm) seam, leaving about 2 in. (5 cm) unstitched, and turn right side out. Press carefully. Stitch the medium circles (1 print and 1 plain) in the same way, turning and pressing carefully. Stitch closed the openings of both circles.

To make a casing for the drawstring, on the large circle sew two parallel rows aligned with the ends of the buttonholes (see diagram 3).

The medium circle will become the inner pockets of the sewing bag. To mark the stitching lines for the pockets, fold the circle in half, then in thirds, then in half again and press—this will give you 12 equal sections.

Mark the centers of the two fabric circles and the plastic circle. Lay down the large fabric circle, plain side up; center the plastic circle on top, then position

the medium fabric circle—print side up—on top of the plastic circle. Check that the middle points line up. Pin the three layers together to hold in place for stitching.

Using the zipper foot on your machine, stitch all around close to the edge of the plastic. Next stitch the pocket sections. Begin at the outside edge of the small circle and stitch toward the center along one of the pressed fold lines, stopping ¾ in. (19 mm) from the stitched line around the plastic. Turn the work and stitch around the arc to the next fold line, turn stitch to the top of the small circle; sew back over this line of stitching as far as the previous arc line of stitching. Repeat until all pockets have been stitched (see diagram 4).

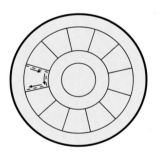

Diagram 4

Thread the ribbon through all the beading lace and the beading header of the gathered edging. Position beading lace on the outside of the bag over the pocket stitching lines and stitch in place down the edges. Then use the ⅜ in. (10 mm) lace to cover the raw edges of the beading at the top and the bottom, taking care not to stitch down the pocket openings on the inside of the bag. Stitch the gathered edging lace around the outside top edge of the bag. Cut the cord in half all the way around and thread each half all the way around through the drawstring casing; add a bead to the ends on each side and then knot the ends together.

Hand-painted Lap Desk

¹¹⁄₁₆ in. (18 mm) thick craft wood: cut to these
dimensions:
Top: 13 x 2¹³⁄₁₆ in. (33 x 7.2 cm)
Lid: 13 x 9⅜ in. (33 x 23.7 cm)
Bottom: 13 x 12 in. (33 x 30.5 cm)
Sides: cut two pieces 11¼ x 3½ in. (28.5 x 9 cm)
Back: 12¼ x 3½ in. (31 x 9 cm)
Front: 12¼ x 2⅝ in. (31 x 6.7 cm)
PVA wood glue
masking tape
clamps (optional)
protractor to mark miter angles
set square, T-square or right triangle
pencil, ruler, saw
2 brass hinges and small brass screws
fine sandpaper
wood sealer
acrylic paints—white, brown, yellow, teal green and
antique green
brushes—No. 6 round, ¼ in. (6 mm) flat,
No. 2 liner
base-coater brush
old base-coating brush
tracing (graphite) paper
transfer paper
stylus
antiquing patina
burnt umber artist's oilpaint
lint-free cloth
rubber gloves
mineral-based spray sealer

Refer to the following instruction to make the lap desk, or purchase a ready-made one.

Diagram 1 shows a side view of the lap desk pieces.

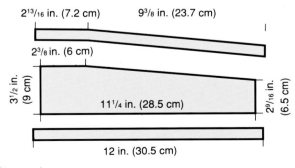

2¹³⁄₁₆ in. (7.2 cm)   9⅜ in. (23.7 cm)

2⅜ in. (6 cm)

3½ in. (9 cm)

11¼ in. (28.5 cm)

2⁹⁄₁₆ in. (6.5 cm)

12 in. (30.5 cm)

Diagram 1

Miter the sides, back and front, with a 45 degree angle. Cut the back edge of the lid at a 5 degree angle and cut the front top edge at 5 degrees also. Molded edges are optional.

Assembly of the Lap Desk

Sand both faces of all pieces. Lay out the sides, back and front as shown in diagram 2 and use masking tape to hold the pieces together.

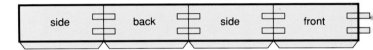

side   back   side   front

Diagram 2

Turn the taped pieces to the other side and apply glue to the joints. Fold to form a box. The masking tape will hold the box together and act as a clamping method. (Clamps may be used if necessary.) Square up the box and leave while the glue sets completely. When the glue is set remove the masking tape and sand the corners and all sides of the box to a smooth finish. Apply glue to the bottom and to the top edges of the box. Leave the slanted top edges free of glue as this is where the lid will sit. Position the box onto the bottom making sure the overhang of the bottom is equal on all sides as shown in diagram 3.

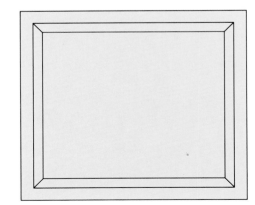

Diagram 3

Put the top on the box and align the top edges with the bottom edges. Make sure that the front edge of the top lines up where the slant starts as shown in diagram 4.

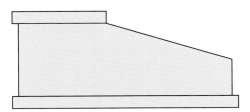

Diagram 4

Clamp together and let the glue set.

Fix the hinges to the top first 1⅜ in. (35 mm) from the side edges. Then line up the lid to the top and screw the hinges onto lid as indicated in diagram 5.

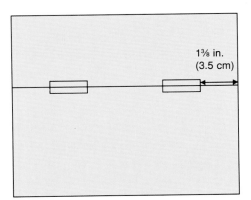

1⅜ in. (3.5 cm)

Diagram 5

Painting Instructions

Seal the inner and outer surfaces of the desk then coat using the base-coater brush and the antique green paint. Leave to dry and then sand lightly.

Trace the patterns and position them in their appropriate positions on the lap desk (refer to the color photograph), as follows: secure the traced pattern with masking tape, slide the transfer paper underneath the pattern and lightly trace over the pattern with the stylus.

Order of painting: 1 dark leaves, 2 roses, 3 medium leaves, 4 round and spiky daisies, 5 light leaves, 6 dot daisies, 7 yellow dots, 8 tendrils.

The comma-shaped leaves are painted with a round brush. The rose leaves are painted with a flat brush, just like coloring-in. Dark leaves are teal green, medium leaves are teal green with a touch of yellow, and the light leaves are yellow with a touch of white.

To paint the roses, load a flat brush with brown and a touch of teal green and pat into the center of the roses. Then load the flat brush with one corner dipped into the brown and the other in the white and paint in the petals at the top of the bowl of the rose using C strokes. Add more brown to the brown side and more white to the white side and paint in the outside petals—push your brush into the ridge of white at the petal's outer edge and pull towards the bowl of the rose. This creates the streaked effect.

With the brush loaded with half brown and half white, paint the center petals to form the bowl of the rose. Paint in the same manner as for outer petals.

Round-petal daisies are painted by loading the round brush with yellow and then dotting it in white. Very lightly press the tip of the brush to the surface painting five small petals on at a time to form the daisy. Add yellow centers.

Spiky daisies are made with a loaded flat brush with one yellow corner and one white corner. Paint each petal by holding the brush upright with all the bristles on the painting surface then pressing down sideways on the white side. Add a yellow center.

To paint the dot daisies, dip the handle end of any brush in the white and press to the surface to form the petals. Add the tendrils with the liner brush. Leave to dry.

For the next stage, it is advisable to wear rubber gloves to protect your hands. Squeeze a little burnt umber oil paint onto the desk. Dip the old base-coating brush into the antiquing patina. Spread the oil paint over the entire outside surface of the desk with the patina-moistened brush, working one surface at a time. Use the lint-free cloth to rub the oil paint and patina until the desired effect is achieved. Leave to dry overnight and then complete by spraying with the mineral-based sealer.

Following pages: Hand-painted Lap Desk.
Flowers were hand painted on many
objects during the Victorian era.

front of lap desk

top of lap desk

top corner of lap desk

White

Brown

Yellow

Teal green

Brazilian Embroidered Jewel Box

20 in. (50 cm) of black chintz cotton fabric
scissors, white dressmaker's carbon paper
stranded embroidery floss—bright green, forest green,
teal, ivory, orange, burnt orange, bright yellow,
bright purple, dark purple, lavender, dark cherry red,
bright cobalt blue
No. 8 milliner's/straw embroidery needle
No. 8 crewel embroidery needle
tracing paper, pencil
thick cardboard
polyester batting (wadding)
spray adhesive, quick-drying craft glue
ruler

1²/₃ yd (1.5 m) of ³/₈ in. (10 mm) wide braid
3¼ yd (3 m) of gold cord
extra cord or braid—optional for the corners

Embroidery stitches used:
stem stitch
wrapped lazy daisy
bullion knot stitch
satin stitch
French knot
fern stitch
Brazilian embroidery—each flower is detailed
individually in the project instructions

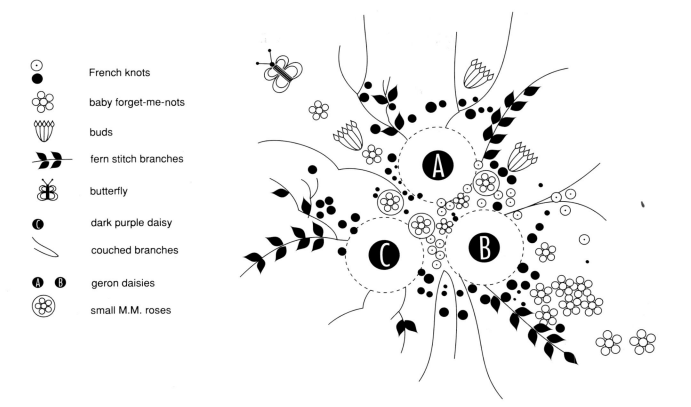

⊙ ●	French knots
🌼	baby forget-me-nots
🌷	buds
➤➤	fern stitch branches
🦋	butterfly
●	dark purple daisy
╱	couched branches
Ⓐ Ⓑ	geron daisies
🌸	small M.M. roses

Cut out a piece of black chintz cotton fabric 10 x 12 in. (25 x 30 cm). Trace the embroidery design and transfer it onto the fabric using the white dressmaker's carbon paper. Work the Brazilian embroidery, according to the symbols, color code and instructions that follow.

Baby forget-me-nots

Use these colors: bright cobalt blue petals, bright yellow centers. Use the No. 8 milliner's/straw needle for the bullion knot stitch and the No. 8 crewel embroidery needle for the other stitches, with one strand of thread only.

Mark the center of the flower and work three French knots. Then work three or four looped bullion stitches around the center, giving each bullion stitch 25 wraps. The stitch is $\frac{1}{32}$ to $\frac{1}{16}$ in. (1 to 2 mm) in length.

Note: In this looped bullion stitch, more wraps are placed on the needle than the stitch length allows, thus forcing the bullion to curve and be detached from the fabric.

Small M. M. Rose

Use pale lavender, No. 8 crewel needle and one strand of thread.

As shown in diagram 1, using a stem stitch to outline and working in an anti-clockwise direction, come up at 1, pull the thread all the way through, then go down at 2, up again at 3 (which is halfway between 1 and 2).

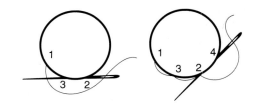

Diagram 1

Note: Make sure the thread is under the needle. Do not pull the thread too tight—an even tension is required. Continue working around this circle with unevenly spaced stitches until the circle is complete.

Opposite: Brazilian Embroidered Jewel Box surrounded by antique jewelry pieces.

Now, with a variation of the stem stitch and working on the inside of the completed circle, start again at 1 (diagram 2) and go exactly halfway around the circle, go down at 2 and back up at 3, which is approximately ³⁄₁₆ in. (5 mm) to ¼ in. (6 mm) from 1, *i.e. t*reating the circle as a clockface: come up at 6 o'clock (1) pull the thread all the way through and go down again at 10 o'clock (2), come up again at 4 o'clock (3) (see diagram 2a); 4 o'clock now becomes (1), go halfway around the clockface to 10 o'clock (2) and come out at 2 o'clock (3) (diagram 2b).

Work at least once around the circle in this manner to fill the flower leaving a small center free of stitching.

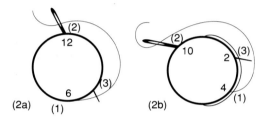

Diagram 2

After each stitch, pull the thread snug but not too tight—this will make the original stem stitches stand up. Fill the center of the flower with French knots.

French Knots

To stitch the French knots, refer to the color illustration on page 74 for placement of the different colors.

For the bright cobalt blue, dark cherry red and bright yellow knots, use the No. 8 crewel embroidery needle and a single strand of floss.

For the bright orange French knots, use two strands of floss.

For the ivory, use two strands of floss and the same embroidery needle.

For the dark purple, again use two strands.

Stitch the stem stitch in dark forest green and bright green, using one strand of floss and the crewel embroidery needle.

Geron Daisies (A and B)

Geron daisy B is made with dark purple pistol-stitch petals and bright yellow French-knot centers.

Geron daisy A has bright purple pistol-stitch petals, lavender pistol-stitch petals and orange French knots for the center.

To stitch a geron daisy, come up at the edge of the circle, wrap the needle and go down at the end of the petal. Be sure to vary the lengths of each petal in each daisy. The variegated geron daisy A is worked with a combination of stem stitches some with French knots at the end and some with wraps. The geron daisy B, worked in bright purple, has small French knots at each end.

Couched Branches

Refer to the instructions in the Stitch Glossary. Use bright green and No. 8 crewel embroidery needle.

Fern-stitch Branches

Stitch the fern stitch branches using both forest green and bright green. Work a stem stitch for the branch and fern stitches at either side.

Butterfly

Stitch the butterfly in burnt orange and teal blue, using the milliner's/straw needle with one strand of thread only. Bullion stitch the body and the wings and pistol stitch the antennae.

The body is three straight bullion stitches in teal. The first stitch has 37 wraps, the middle has 40 wraps and the third has 37 wraps.

The head is four small satin stitches using teal.

The antennae, in teal, are stitched with pistol stitch, and couched to create the curve. The stitch length is ¼ in. (6 mm), with three wraps on the end.

The wings are attached at the body only. Use burnt orange for the inner top wing, giving 25 wraps, and teal for the top outer wing, with 60 wraps; burnt orange for the bottom inner wing, with 50 wraps, and teal for the bottom outer wing, giving 80 wraps.

Dark Purple Daisy (C)

The dark purple daisy (C) is stitched as a lazy daisy with wraps at the end; the center is satin stitched.

For the petals, use one strand of floss only and the No. 8 crewel embroidery needle. Refer to diagram 3. Come up at A, bring the thread all the way through.

Go back slightly to the right of A and in at B and come out at C. Do not bring the needle all the way through yet. Wrap the point of the needle 9 or 10 times and then pull through. Take the needle down again at D.

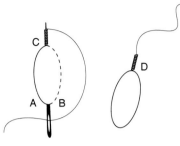

Diagram 3

The flower can have between 18 and 20 petals, depending on the size of the center circle.

Buds

The buds are worked with a bullion stitch calyx of 15 wraps with 5 to 7 petals, using one strand of dark purple thread and a No. 8 crewel embroidery needle.

Making the Embroidered Lid

Use the completed embroidery for the jewel box lid. To make the box, first enlarge the scaled patterns as instructed on page 4. Transfer the patterns onto the thick cardboard. Cut out carefully.

Apply polyester batting (wadding) to the two lid pieces and the outside of the four flaps of the base, using spray adhesive. Trim any excess from the edges.

Cut out the black chintz for each piece with a 1⅛ in. (3 cm) allowance all round, cutting the larger lid piece from the completed embroidery.

Be sure to position the embroidery correctly before spray-gluing that piece of fabric to the batting (wadding) covered side of the larger lid piece. Glue the fabric over to the back. Then, using the craft glue, stick the corners of the fabric to the cardboard; press down firmly until the fabric adheres to the cardboard. Glue all four sides in the same way. Glue the ⅜ in. (10 mm) wide braid around the edge of the top of the lid. Glue the gold cord along the inside edge of the braid. Spread craft glue on the back of the smaller, inside lid piece and stick it to the center of the cardboard side of the outside lid.

Completing the Box

Score the four fold lines for the sides of the box carefully using the point of the scissors. Spray-glue the fabric you cut out for the base of the box to the batting (wadding) covered side.

Spray-adhere the batting (wadding) side of the cardboard onto the center of the fabric. Snip into the four corners of the box, stopping ¹⁄₁₆ in. (2 mm) from the edge of the cardboard (diagram 4).

Glue the fabric over onto the cardboard, holding firmly until dry. Fold up the sides of the box and run a line of quick-drying glue down the edges where the corners meet. You may like to cover the corner joins with braid or cord.

Cut a piece of batting (wadding) the same size as the bottom of the box and glue this on the bottom inside the box. Cut a piece of the black chintz slightly larger than the bottom of the box and glue this in the bottom and partly up the sides. Using a ruler, measure each side of the inside of the box and cut out cardboard pieces to the exact measurements of the sides.

Cover one side of each piece with batting (wadding) and then with fabric. Cut the fabric ¾ in. (3 cm) larger all round and lightly spray-glue to fasten it to the cardboard: fold in and glue the corners and then all four edges. Then glue the four covered side panels inside the box with the craft glue.

Decorate the outside of the box by gluing the ⅜ in. (10 mm) wide braid around the base, then the gold cord against the top edge of the braid, then another row of the gold cord ⅜ in. (10 mm) above that. Glue the gold cord around the top edge of the box, too. Then cap it with the embroidered lid.

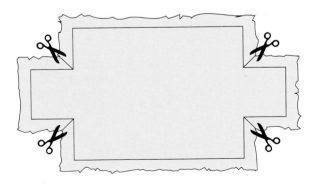

Diagram 4

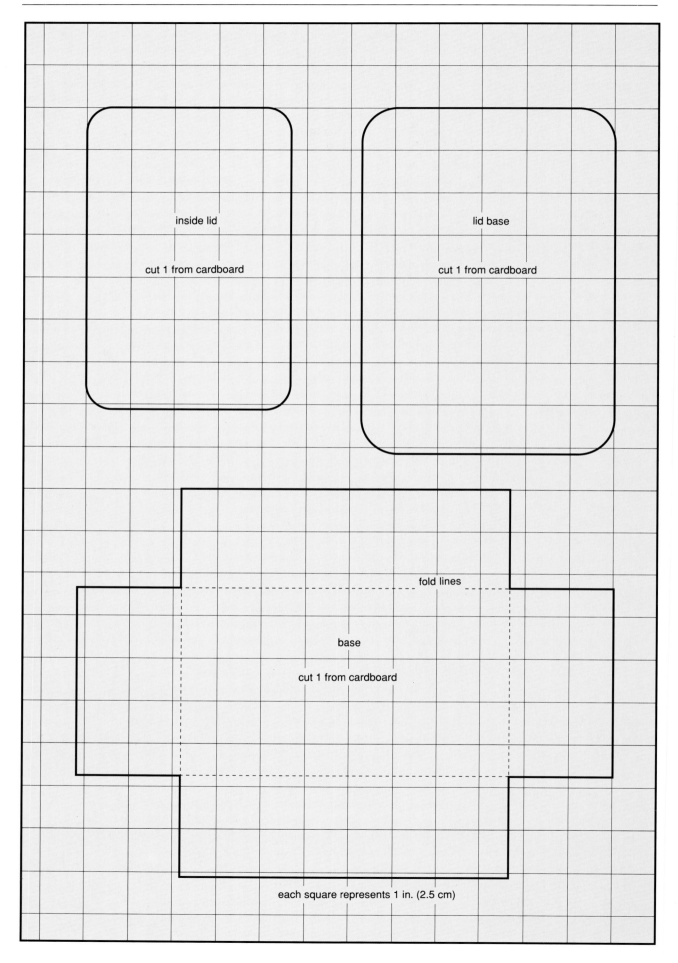

inside lid

cut 1 from cardboard

lid base

cut 1 from cardboard

fold lines

base

cut 1 from cardboard

each square represents 1 in. (2.5 cm)

My Diary

hard-cover diary 6¼ x 8¼ in. (16 x 21 cm)
approximately
13¾ x 9⅞ in. (35 x 25 cm) of natural noil silk
No. 20 tapestry needle
tracing (graphite) paper
pencil, scissors
No. 20 chenille needle
stranded floss in assorted colors
⅛ in. (3 mm) wide silk ribbons in assorted colors
polyester batting (wadding)
spray adhesive
quick-drying craft glue

Embroidery stitches used:
ribbon stitch
French knot
straight stitch
colonial knot
twisted chain stitch—roses
rosebuds
whipped running stitch

Open the diary in half and lay it on the fabric. Cut out the fabric allowing 1⅛ in. (3 cm) extra around the edges. Transfer the design onto the fabric, using the tracing (graphite) paper, being sure to center it on the front of the diary. All stitches are done with the chenille needle except the wrapping stitch in the whipped running stitch, which uses the tapestry needle.

Using the chenille needle, work a row of running stitches along the words "My Diary". The stitches should be even in length and each stitch should be slightly longer than the width of the ribbon used. The gaps between each stitch should be as small as you can comfortably make them.

Using a tapestry needle, begin wrapping the ribbon just before the start of the first running stitch (see diagram 1): spread the ribbon and with the ribbon below the needle pass the needle down under the first running stitch. Repeat a second time through the same stitch. Tighten this stitch to wrap firmly around the foundation stitch.

For best results take care to remove all twists from the ribbon and ensure that the full face of the ribbon

wraps flat around the running stitches. Pass the needle under the second running stitch in the same way but take care not to pull this stitch too firmly or allow the ribbon to twist (diagram 2). Firmly wrap this foundation stitch a second time as before. Continue this sequence along the line of running stitches alternating tightly wrapped stitches around the foundation stitching with more loosely wrapped stitches between each foundation stitch.

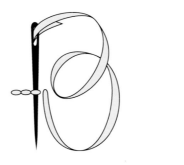

Diagram 1   Diagram 2

To embroider the roses, work a colonial knot for the center rose. Then place three twisted chain stitches in a neat circle around the knot. Pull the needle through the fabric at point A (see diagram 3).

Form a small anticlockwise loop and pass the needle down through point B, level with, but to the left of, point A. Bring the needle back up at point C inside the loop of ribbon and immediately below point A. The distance between points A and C will depend on the thickness of the ribbon. It works best when this distance is equal to the width of the ribbon being used.

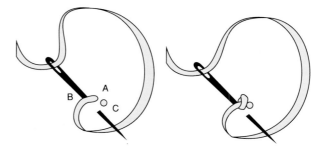

Diagram 3

The daily ritual of diary-writing was enjoyed by many Victorian women.

The rose can be finished at this point, or for a larger flower work a second circle of four or five twisted chain stitches so that it touches, but does not overlap, the previous stitches.

Next stitch the straight-stitch stems and then the rosebuds in the top corner and the rosebuds along the curve of the Y.

Working from the base to the tip of the bud, lay a single straight stitch of equal length to the width of the ribbon being used. Cover this stitch with a second straight stitch starting immediately below and extending just beyond the tip of the first stitch. Using a single strand of embroidery floss, two shades darker than the ribbon, come up at the base of the bud and take a single straight stitch two thirds of the way up the center of the ribbon stitch. Bring the needle back up on the left-hand side of the bud, in line with this point. Take the needle down on the right-hand side of the bud and out at the base, with the thread looped under the needle. Anchor with a tiny straight stitch or use this thread to form a stem for the bud (see diagram 4).

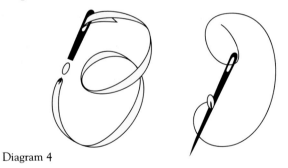

Diagram 4

Stitch the three buds above the top corner roses with twisted chain stitch and ribbon stitch leaves. Bring the needle up at A. Making sure that the ribbon is flat and straight on the fabric in the direction you want it to go, hold it in place with your left thumb and take the needle back through the ribbon at B (see diagram 5). Pull the needle through to the back of the work. Still holding the ribbon with your left thumb,

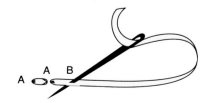

Diagram 5

pull the ribbon until the lip starts to curl back on itself and forms the point. Try not to pull the stitch too tightly—this will result in a very tight and thin stitch.

Work the petals and leaves of the flowers at the beginning of the M with straight stitch and French knots in the centers. To produce well-shaped, even knots when stitching with ribbon, always neaten the ribbon around the shaft of the needle while the needle is held in a perpendicular position in the fabric and before completing the last step. The leaves around the roses in the wording are all ribbon stitch. The flowers on the D are straight-stitch daisies. The French knots are done in the different colors as desired. The dot of the I is a colonial knot.

Cut a piece of batting (wadding) to fit the outside cover of the diary. Spray-adhere the batting (wadding) to the diary and trim back any overlapping edges.

Lay the fabric out flat, with the embroidered side facing down. Spray-glue the batting (wadding) on the back cover of the diary and attach it to the plain half of the fabric, positioning it with the extra 1 1/8 in. (2.8 cm) around the edges. Glue the front cover in the same way.

Open the diary to the inside front cover. Bring the two corners and the side fabric over onto the inside cover and stick down with craft glue. Make two small cuts in the fabric, near the top and bottom of the center binding as shown in diagram 6. Glue the top and bottom fabric onto the inside cover. Repeat the process for the inside back cover.

Trim back the remaining fabric flaps at the top and bottom of the spine. To complete, glue the first page of the diary to the inside front cover and the last page to the inside back cover, with craft glue.

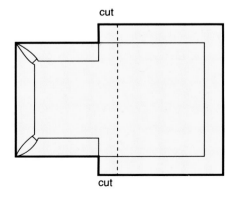

Diagram 6

Writing Compendium

thick cardboard
scissors
pencil, ruler
20 in. (50 cm) of 45 in. (115 cm) wide fabric
spray adhesive
polyester batting (wadding)
quick-drying craft glue
1²/₃ yd (1.5 m) gold braid
matching paper and envelopes

Accurately draw and cut out two pieces of cardboard 11 x 8 in. (28 x 20 cm) for the outside cover and two pieces measuring 10 ⁵/₈ x 7 ⁷/₈ in. (27 x 20 cm) for the inside cover. For side pieces, cut two 10 ⁵/₈ x 3 in. (27 x 7.5 cm) in size, and one each for the outside and inside center measuring 11 x 1 in. (28 x 2.5 cm) and 10 ⁵/₈ x 1 in. (27 x 2.5 cm).

To make it easier follow the exact measurements displayed on the scaled-down drawings of each piece

The Victorian lady's Writing Compendium was used to store letters and invitations as well as fine imported paper.

shown in diagram 1 and cut out the eight pieces. (Patterns can be drawn—full size—for repeated use.)

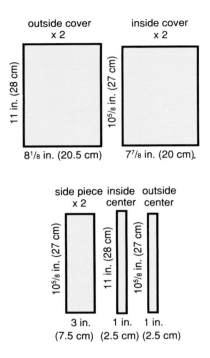

Diagram 1

Arrange the cardboard pieces on the fabric, placing the larger outside center piece in between the two outside cover pieces. Leave a $1/16$ in. (2 mm) gap between the pieces.

Cut out the fabric, allowing $1\frac{1}{8}$ in. (3 cm) extra around the edges, as illustrated in diagram 2.

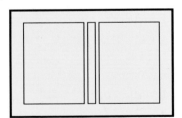

Diagram 2

Cut out the fabric for the inside cover the same way as for the outside cover—refer to diagram 2.

Spray the outside cover pieces with adhesive and position them on the polyester batting (wadding), again the same distance apart as they were placed for cutting. Trim back the batting (wadding) on the outside edges of the cardboard.

Spray-adhere the outside cover pieces, batting

(wadding) side down, onto the fabric the same as they were placed for cutting the fabric. Glue and fold over the corners and then the sides of the fabric onto the cardboard side with craft glue, as illustrated in diagram 3. Do the same for the inside cover pieces.

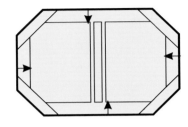

Diagram 3

Cut the fabric for the two side pieces, allowing 2 in. (5 cm) of fabric extra all around each cardboard piece. Glue the two cardboard side pieces to the fabric. Glue and fold over one edge of the fabric only—see diagram 4. Decorate this edge with gold braid, using glue to adhere.

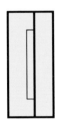

Diagram 4

Place each side piece, fabric side out, on top of the fabric side of the inside cover, matching the outer edges of the cardboard and with the finished-off side facing inwards—diagram 5.

Carefully turn the inside cover over, holding the side pieces in place. Glue the extra top and bottom fabric of the side pieces over onto the cardboard sides of the inside cover, as shown in diagram 5.

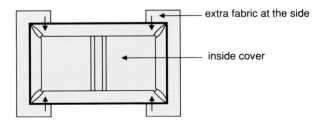

Diagram 5

84

Cut off the corners of the side fabric, then glue the long edges onto the cardboard side of the inside cover.

Apply glue around the edge of the cardboard side of the inside cover and attach this to the cardboard side of the outside cover. Carefully line up the two center pieces and, before the glue has time to dry, check that the whole will fold. Refer to the photographs of the open and closed Writing Compendium for placement of the gold braid. Use glue to adhere. Fill the pockets made by the side pieces with matching envelopes and paper, and the Writing Compendium is complete.

The inside of the Writing Compendium.

Bead-embroidered Wrist Bag

pencil
tracing (graphite) paper
17¾ x 45¼ in. (45 x 115 cm) ivory raw silk
scissors, pins, iron
No. 9 crewel embroidery needle
beading needle
ivory sewing floss
No. 8 milliner's/straw needle
Marlitt floss No. 1212
¹⁄₁₆ in. (2 mm) ivory colored "pearls"
sewing machine
17¾ x 9½ in. (45 x 24 cm) Pellon
ivory "seed pearls"
30 ivory "drop pearls"
39 in. (1 m) of ⅛ in. (3 mm) thick cording
1³⁄₁₆ in. (3 cm) white wooden bead
quick-drying craft glue

Embroidery stitches used:
  bullion stitch
  couching stitch
  French knot

Trace the pattern for the bag cuff and cut out four pieces from the fabric (two are for the lining). Trace the embroidery design and transfer across the entire peaked edge of the cuff in a repeat onto two pieces of the fabric, using the tracing (graphite) paper.

Embroider the design and sew the beads on according to the pattern. (Do not sew on the beads at the peaked edge of the cuff; these are sewn on later.)

Follow the legend on the embroidery design for stitch placement. The buds are stitched in a bullion stitch with two strands of Marlitt floss No. 1212 using the No. 8 milliner's/straw needle . Referring to diagram 1, make two bullions side by side with 12 wraps each. The third, fourth and fifth bullions have 17 wraps each. Then stitch two either side at the top of the bud with 17 wraps each.

Diagram 1

Stitch the French knots and the couched branches with one strand of Marlitt floss using the No. 9 crewel embroidery needle.

With the right sides of the fabric together, machine stitch one of the embroidered pieces of fabric to one of the lining pieces, following the stitching guide in diagram 2.

Turn right sides out and press. Repeat for the other piece of the cuff.

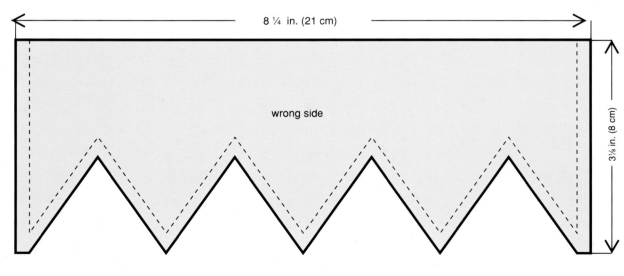

8 ¼ in. (21 cm)

wrong side

3⅛ in. (8 cm)

Diagram 2

A Bead-embroidered Wrist Bag like this one was kept for special occasions.

Enlarge the scaled pattern for the outer bag and cut two pieces of fabric and two pieces of Pellon. Pin the fabric on top of the Pellon and straight stitch 14 rows along each side of the fabric, leaving the middle of each piece plain. Finish the rows at the line marked on the pattern. The first row is ⅜ in. (10 mm) from each outside long edge of the fabric. Work inwards at ³⁄₁₆ in. (5 mm) spacing.

Transfer the pattern for the placement of beads (diagram 3) onto the bag 3⅛ in. (8 cm) below the marked line and centered in the plain band. Stitch the beads on using the beading needle.

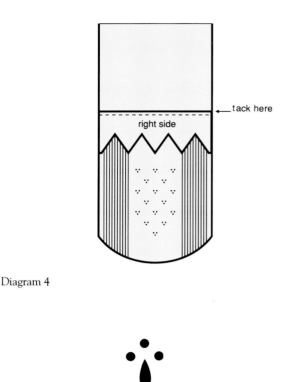

Diagram 4

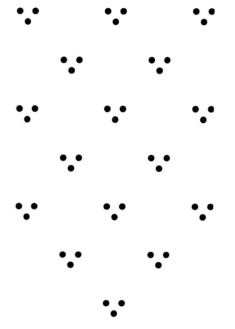

Diagram 3

Place the two lined bag pieces right sides together and stitch the bottom seams together, then stitch the side seams together; note the two different seam allowances.

Position the cuff around the center of the bag with the wrong side of the cuff against the right side of the bag, where indicated on the outer bag pattern. Each side of the cuff will overlap slightly. Tack the cuff in place along the top edge (see diagram 4).

Cut a strip of fabric 2 x 16½ in. (5 x 42 cm), fold in half lengthwise and press. Align the raw edge with the top of the cuff and stitch where the previous seam is. Adjust the piece so that the seam line is centered underneath it and press to hold the folded edges. Stitch on the beads around the fabric strip in the

Diagram 5

formation as shown in diagram 5 and spaced at 2 in. (5 cm) intervals.

Cut two pieces of fabric for the lining 8¼ x 12¼ in. (21 x 31 cm). Use the pattern for the bag to give the bottom shaping. Stitch the bottom together, then stitch the side seams, leaving ⅜ in. (10 mm) seam allowance. Leave wrong side out and place it inside the bag.

Turn the top edge of the bag back 1¾ in. (4.5 cm) and turn the raw edge under ³⁄₁₆ in. (5 mm). Make sure the turn-back covers the top of the lining. Pin in place, then stitch 1 in. (2.5 cm) from the top edge. Stitch another row 1⅝ in. (4 cm) from the top edge, making a casing for the cord. Snip the stitches in the outside seam on both sides to make openings for the cord between the stitched rows of the casing.

Stitch the beads to the peaked edges of the cuff, placing a drop bead on each of the peaks. Stitch each bead individually, making sure they are evenly spaced; then secure each bead with a second stitch between it and the next. Thread the cord through, extending it out both openings to form a drawstring.

Smear the wooden bead with glue and push the ¹⁄₁₆ in. (2 mm) ivory pearls onto it in rows until completely covered. Cut five 20 in. (50 cm) lengths of thread. Thread each onto a beading needle and distribute the length evenly so that it becomes a doubled 10 in. (25 cm) length. Thread the ivory pearls on until there is a 6¼ in. (16 cm) length of pearls.

Double the lengths of pearls into loops and insert the ends through the wooden bead as shown in diagram 6.

Tie the ends into a neat knot close to the bead. Attach the beaded tassel to the center bottom of the bag by stitching through the knotted ends.

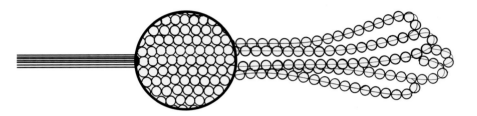

Diagram 6

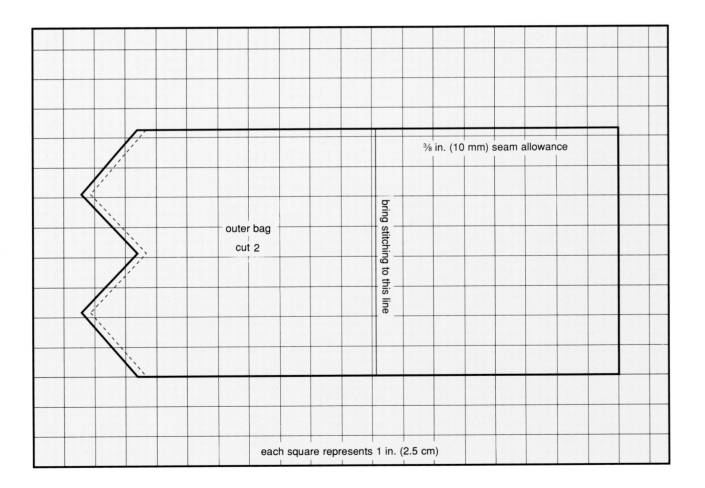

⅜ in. (10 mm) seam allowance

outer bag

cut 2

bring stitching to this line

each square represents 1 in. (2.5 cm)

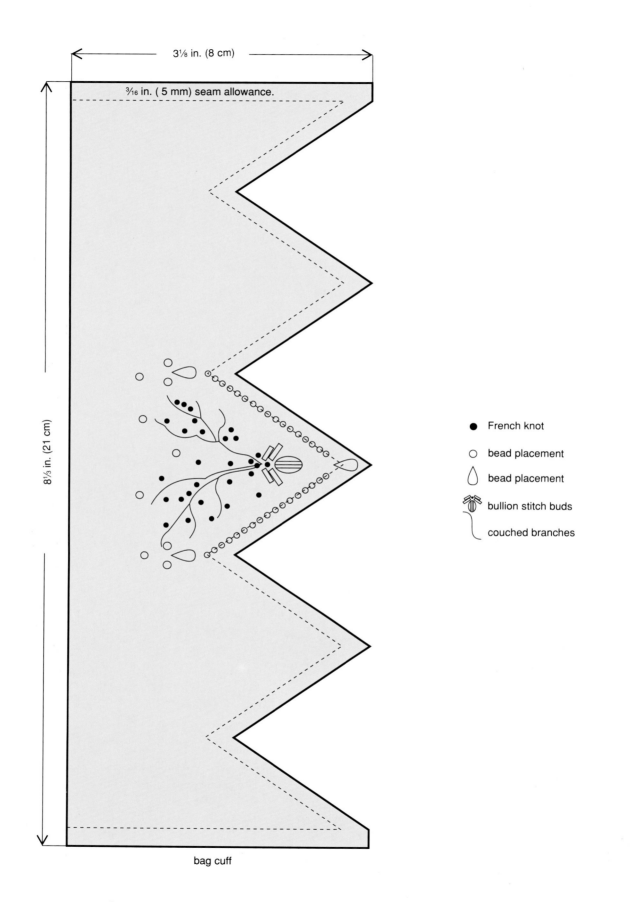

3⅛ in. (8 cm)

³⁄₁₆ in. (5 mm) seam allowance.

8⅓ in. (21 cm)

bag cuff

● French knot

○ bead placement

◊ bead placement

bullion stitch buds

couched branches

Victorian Lady's Fan

12 in. (30.5 cm) paper fan
approximately 12 x 25½ in. (30.5 x 65 cm) of fabric
or lace
pencil, scissors, tape measure
spray adhesive
quick-drying craft glue
parafilm (florist's tape)
florist's wire
lace, ribbons, pearls, dried and silk flowers,
braid as desired for decorating

Open the fan out as flat as possible. Carefully pull the wooden piece off the right-hand side of the fan (if the paper is ripped slightly the fan can still be used). The fan will now flatten out completely. Lay the fan on the fabric or lace and draw around with the pencil, allowing 1 in. (2.5 cm) extra around the top of the fan, 2 in. (5 cm) at the sides and the exact shape of the fan on the inner arc. Cut out the fabric along the pencil lines. Spray the wrong side of the fabric or lace and the paper fan with adhesive. Lay the fabric on the right side of the fan, leaving about 1⅛ in. (3 cm) of extra fabric on the left-hand edge, and smooth down the fabric so it adheres to the fan. Trim back the fabric around the top edge of the fan and on the right-hand side. Trim the left-hand side leaving ⅜ in. (10 mm) of fabric and use adhesive to attach it around to the back of the fan.

Pleat the fan back into its original shape and decorate with lace and ribbon as desired. To determine the lengths of braid needed, measure first and cut to size; then glue the pieces on with quick-drying craft glue. Pre-gathered laces can be glued onto the back of the fan so they can extend beyond the edge. Make up posies using the dried flowers, pearls, ribbons, tassels, and lace ribbons, wire together and cover the stems with florist's tape. Use the wire to hold the posy in place at the base of the fan, and squeeze a few dabs of glue on to give extra hold.

The Victorian Lady's Fan shown in two different styles.

CHAPTER 3

Decorating the Home

Ornate furnishings in distinctive colors and patterns are reminiscent of the decor in homes of the Victorian era. Heavy ornate furniture and rich floral fabrics and wallpapers provided the mainstays of decorating, with an abundance of nicknacks, framed pictures, patterned china, cushions, pretty lamp-shades and adornments wherever possible.

The people of the era found much joy in spending their leisure time at home, both enjoying their warm, pleasant surroundings and making yet more intricate needlework articles to embellish further their already abundantly filled homes.

Above: Victorian Cat Cushion.
Opposite: From left, Victorian Lady's Fan, Topiary Tree, Floral Lampshade,
Candlewick Cushion, Victorian Cat Cushion and Découpage pieces.

Hat Boxes

thick cardboard
pencil, ruler, compass
scissors, pins
fusible webbing or spray adhesive
fabric
iron
quick-drying craft glue
polyester batting (wadding)
pins
trims—braid, fringe and cord for decoration

Precut the cardboard pieces required:

Small Hat Box	
Lid band	1½ x 32¾ in. (3.8 x 83 cm)
Base band	5⅞ x 32¾ in. (15 x 83 cm)
Lid	9⅞ in. (25 cm) diameter circle
Base	9⅞ in. (25 cm) diameter circle
Medium Hat Box	
Lid Band	1½ x 39 in. (3.8 cm x 1 m)
Base band	7⅛ x 39 in. (18 cm x 1 m)
Lid	11⅞ in. (30 cm) diameter circle
Base	11⅞ in. (30 cm) diameter circle
Large Hat Box	
Lid band	1⅝ x 47⅝ in. (4 cm x 1.21 m)
Base band	8½ x 47⅝ in. (21.5 cm x 1.21 m)
Lid	14¾ in. (37.5 cm) diameter circle
Base	14¾ in. (37.5 cm) diameter circle

Draw the necessary shapes onto cardboard and carefully cut out. There are four pieces of cardboard for each box.

Cut the fusible webbing for the bands 1⅝ in. (4 cm) wider and longer than the cardboard pieces. Draw around the lid on fusible webbing and cut with an additional ¾ in. (19 mm) allowance all the way around. Draw around the base and cut the fusible webbing to the exact size. These are for the outside fabric; mark each piece with a pencil.

Cut another set of fusible webbing for the box band, the lid band and the circular part of the lid to the exact size. Draw around the base and cut out webbing allowing ¾ in. (19 mm) extra all round. Mark the pieces with a pencil; these are for the inside.

Lay the fusible webbing, paper side up, on the wrong side of the fabrics to be used. Work on a large flat surface. Position each piece according to the design on the fabric. Pay attention to how the design will appear on the finished box. Fuse the webbing to the fabric using the iron, according to the manufacturer's instructions. Carefully cut out the fabric along the edges of the fusible webbing. Leave the paper backing on until you are ready to use each piece of fabric. Do not discard the paper. Put the paper under each matching pattern piece so that you do not iron the fabric to the ironing board.

Alternatively, you can apply the fabric to the cardboard pieces with spray adhesive and use craft glue to attach the turned-under fabric edges.

Outside Box Band

Position the base band of the box in the middle of the wrong side of the fabric, as shown in diagram 1. Notch the corners of the fabric to the edge of the cardboard (diagram 2). Carefully turn the fabric and cardboard over, being careful not to let the fabric slip from its position on the cardboard. Iron the fabric to the cardboard according to the manufacturer's instructions, using the paper to protect the ironing surface. Turn the band over and press the top edge seam allowance and end seam allowances to the band. Clip the remaining seam allowance (the bottom) at ¾ in. (19 mm) intervals along the entire length of the band; clip to the edge of the cardboard.

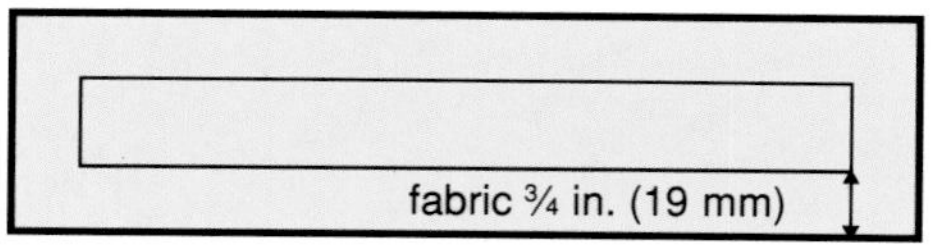

Diagram 1

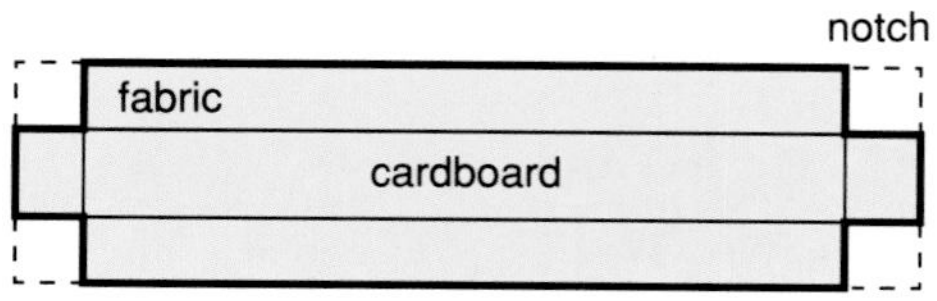

Diagram 2

Outside Lid Band

Follow the instructions given for the box band, but fuse all seam allowances to the band.

Hat Boxes can be used to store many items and keepsakes other than hats.

Inside Box Band

Center the fabric over the inside of the box band. The fabric should be the same size as, or slightly smaller than, the band. It should never be larger. Put paper over the band and iron the fabric in place. The clipped allowance on the bottom of the outside fabric should still be free, as shown in diagram 3.

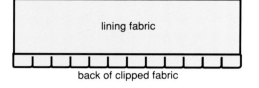

back of clipped fabric

Diagram 3

Inside Lid Band

Center the fabric over the inside of the lid band. Fuse in place. There should be no free seam allowances.

To Make the Lid

Cut a layer of polyester batting (wadding) the exact size of the lid. Glue to the top of the lid. (The batting (wadding) can be ironed on with fusible webbing for a smoother finish.) Place the lid, batting (wadding) side down, on the wrong side of the outside lid fabric. The lid should be centered, leaving a seam allowance of ¾ in. (19 mm) all the way around. Fuse in place. Clip the seam allowance at ¾ in. (19 mm) intervals all the way tot he edge of the cardboard. Lay the lid fabric side down and, pulling gently on the fabric tabs, fuse the tabs to the cardboard. When finished, the fabric should be pulled smooth and firm on the top.

Center the inside fabric on the cardboard side of the lid and fuse in place. Make sure that the edges are well fused.

To assemble the lid, form the lid band around the lid piece as firmly as possible. Mark the overlap with pins. Remove the band and apply quick-drying craft glue to the overlap and hold together firmly until dry.

Insert the lid piece into the band to the top edge and glue in place. Use pins to hold until dry.

To Assemble the Base

Follow the instructions given for the lid, except for the batting (wadding); however, here the larger piece of fabric will be used inside the box. Fuse it directly to the circular cardboard. The smaller circle of the fabric will be used to finish the outside of the base. Do not attach it yet.

Work on a flat surface. Form the side band around the base piece as firmly as possible, being careful not to crease the band or the base. Mark the overlap with pins at the top, middle and bottom points of the band. Remove the band from the base.

Make sure that the overlap is even at all three points to ensure a properly shaped box. Apply the quick-drying craft glue to the overlap and hold together firmly until dry. Fuse the tabs to the cardboard base all the way around. Make sure that the tabs are pulled firmly over the edge and fused flat. Center the base lining fabric over the base and fuse in place. Make sure that the edges are well fused.

Insert the circular base into the shaped band (which now forms the box). Make sure that the inside of the base is on the inside of the box. Work the base to the bottom edge of the band and insert pins through the band into the side of the base to hold in place (diagram 4).

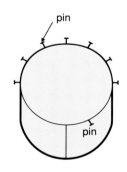

pin

pin

Diagram 4

Finishing

To decorate the boxes, measure the areas to be covered and cut the trims to the required lengths.

Braids and cords can be used to decorate the lower edge of the base band and the lid band; fringe can also be used to give your hat box a more elaborate look. To apply braid and cord around the lid bands and base bands, carefully run a thin line of craft glue where you wish to place them and firmly press in place. Apply fringe to the outside edge of the lid band with glue, then glue a thick cord over the header of the fringe to make it look more finished.

Raffia Hat

approximately 10½ oz (300 g) raffia
1 wool needle or size 14 tapestry needle
iron
wet cloth
about 1 yd (1 m) of 20 in. (50 cm) wide tulle
about 1 yd (1 m) of 1 in. (2.5 cm) wide double-sided satin ribbon
about 1 yd (1 m) of 2⅜ in. (6 cm) wide lace ribbon
8 pieces of colored organza, 14 x 4 in. (35 x 10 cm)
quick-drying craft glue
green silk leaves
small white dried flowers

* If you prefer, you can purchase a straw hat and decorate that instead of making the hat out of raffia.

Count 25 strands of raffia and tie together in a tight bundle using a strong piece of raffia. Tie a loop in it that can be used to attach your bundle to something while plaiting. Divide the 25 strands into 5 equal bunches, then weave the far right bunch over the next, under the third, over the fourth and under the last bunch (see diagram 1).

Diagram 1

As you weave, be sure to keep pulling the weaver bunch out and away from the other bunches to avoid tangling as you plait.

Return to your far right bunch and plait that across in the same manner, separating it from the others as you weave. Press the plait down firmly with your thumbs as you weave to make sure it stays flat.

As your strands begin to thin out, you must join in new strands to keep your plait one continuous length and uniform thickness. Position new strands in with the weaver bunch and hold as you work (diagram 2).

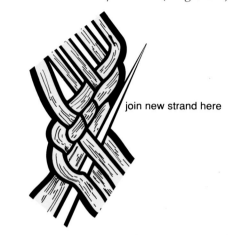

join new strand here

Diagram 2

Plait 3 or 4 yards (2.7 to 3.6 m) initially, then begin stitching the crown of the hat. The finished hat will require between 8 and 10 yards (7.3 to 9.1) of braid (plaiting) but it is easier to begin stitching the crown at this point. Before beginning, trim the untidy ends and then press the plait flat with a hot iron and wet cloth.

Twist the beginning of your plait into a tight spiral, without any gaps. Stitch the beginning of the plait under so that it will lie inside the crown of the hat. The stitching will be on the outer-side of the hat, but if the stitches are neat and uniform, it will look fine. Stitch with a strong piece of raffia in a simple overhand stitch, catching each plait strand as you go (see diagram 3).

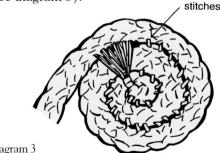

stitches

Diagram 3

To shape the crown so that it is slightly rounded, gently ease the braid a little less and let it take a slight angle down as you stitch; this is a very slight angle for each round of plait. Keep trying the hat on as you work to ensure that it is the correct size and shape.

The Raffia Hat can be displayed on a hat stand or worn to shade the face from the sun.

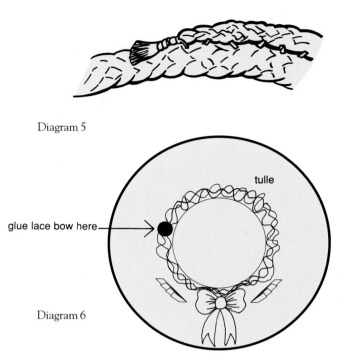

Diagram 5

glue lace bow here———→

tulle

Diagram 4

Diagram 6

To make the sides of the crown, continue gently easing the plait in the same way until you are happy with the shape (diagram 4).

For the brim, simply sew the rounds on a flat surface to make sure that the stitching allows the brim to lie flat. Bend the first round of the brim back against itself to create a sharp edge—you are now stitching on the underside of the brim. Ease the plait slightly as you stitch. Continue until the brim is the width you like.

To finish off, allow the plait to grow thinner as you approach a point of symmetry on your final round of stitching. This is very important because your hat will look lopsided if you finish it off in the wrong place. Taper the plait by dropping out some of the strands in each bunch until they are very thin. Bring it down to a 3-strand braid, then tightly bind off the last ½ in. (13 mm) and stitch it down carefully to the edge of the brim (as in diagram 5).

Fold the tulle in half and drape softly around the crown of the hat; glue in place. Fold the 1 in. (2.5 cm) wide ribbon into three bows and glue onto the hat brim at the back of the crown as shown in diagram 6.

Fold and tie a bow with the ⅜ in. (10 mm) wide lace ribbon and then glue onto the brim as marked on diagram 6.

To make an organza rose, lay a piece of organza on a flat surface and rub your finger down one long edge repeatedly until it begins to curl. Alternatively you can roll-and-whip stitch the edge.

After you have either curled or sewn the top long edge, run a gathering stitch along the other long edge. Pull up the gathering thread and twist the organza into a flower shape. Stitch to secure.

Glue the organza flowers and the silk leaves onto the hat over the folded ribbons and tulle. Glue the small dried flowers into the arrangement.

Crocheted Shelf Liner

3 balls DMC Cebelia No. 10
No. 8 steel crochet hook
(metric 1.5; English 4½)

Tension = 11 dc to 1 in. (2.5 cm)

Abbreviations and Symbols:

dc = double crochet
sc = single crochet
sk = skip
ch(s) = chain
sl st = slip stitch
lp(s) = loop(s)
() Parentheses are used to enclose instructions that should be worked the exact number of times specified after the parentheses.

Row 1. 51 ch. Turn
Row 2. 3 ch (count as 1 dc); (6 dc into next ch) 6 times; 5 ch, sk 5 ch, (1 dc into next ch) 3 times; 5 ch, sk 5 ch, (3 dc, 1 ch, 1 dc) into next ch; 3 ch, sk 2 ch, (1 dc into next ch) 3 times; (2 ch, sk 2 ch, 1 dc into next ch) 6 times; (1 dc into next dc) 6 times; turn.

Row 3. 9 ch; 1 dc into 5th ch from hook, (1 dc into next ch) 4 times; 1 dc into next dc; (2 ch, sk 2 dc, 1 dc into next dc) twice; (2 dc into 2 ch lp, 1 dc into next dc) 4 times; (2 ch, 1 dc into next dc) twice; (2 dc into next dc) twice; 3 ch, (3 dc, 1 ch, 1 dc) into 1 ch lp; 5 ch, sk 3 dc and 5 ch lp, (1 dc into next dc) 3 times; 5 ch, (1 dc into next dc) 7 times; turn.

Row 4. 3 ch (count as a dc); (1 dc into next dc) 6 times; 4 ch, 1 sc into center of 5 ch lps of previous 2 rows (*bow made*); 4 ch, (1 dc into next dc) 3 times; 4 ch, 1 sc into center of 5 ch lps of previous 2 rows (*2nd bow made*); 4 ch, (3 dc, 1 ch, 1 dc) into 1 ch lp; 3 ch, sk 3 dc and 3 ch lp, (1 dc into next dc) 3 times; 2 ch, 1 dc into next dc; 2 dc into 2 ch lp; (1 dc into

Crocheted Shelf Liners are used to decorate plain mantelpieces.

next dc) 4 times; (2 ch, sk 2 ch, 1 dc into next dc) twice; (1 dc into next dc) 3 times; 2 dc into 2 ch lp, 1 dc into next dc; 2 ch, sk 2 ch lp, (1 dc into next dc) 7 times; turn.

Row 5. 9 ch; 1 dc into 5th ch from hook; (1 dc into next dc) 4 times; 1 dc into next dc (2 ch, sk 2 ch, 1 dc into next dc) twice; 2 dc into 2 ch lp, (1 dc into next dc) 4 times; 2 ch, sk 2 dc, 1 dc into next dc, (2 ch, sk 2 ch, 1 dc into next dc) twice; 2 ch, sk 2 dc, (1 dc into next dc) 4 times; 2 ch, (1 dc into next dc) 3 times; 3 ch, (3 dc, 1 ch, 1 dc) into 1 ch lp; 5 ch, sk 3 dc and bow (1 dc into next dc) 3 times; 5 ch, sk bow, (1 dc into next dc) 7 times; turn.

Row 6. 3 ch (count as 1 dc); (1 dc into next dc) 6 times; 5 ch, (1 dc into next dc) 3 times; 5 ch, (3 dc, 1 ch, 1 dc) into 1 ch lp; 3 ch (1 dc into next dc) 3 times; 2 ch, (1 dc into next dc) 4 times; 2 ch, sk 2 ch, 1 dc into next ch; (2 dc into 2 ch lp, 1 dc into next dc) twice; 2 ch, 1 dc into next dc; 2 ch, sk 2 ch (1 dc into next dc) 4 times; 2 dc into 2 ch lp, 1 dc into next dc; 2 ch, sk 2 ch, (1 dc into next dc) 7 times; turn.

Row 7. 9 ch, 1 dc into 5th ch from hook; (1 dc into next ch) 4 times; 1 dc into next dc; (2 ch, sk 2 dc, 1 dc into next dc) twice; 2 dc into 2 ch lp, (1 dc into next dc) 4 times; 2 ch, sk 2 dc, 1 dc into next dc; (2 ch, sk 2 ch, 1 dc into next dc) twice; (1 dc into next dc) 3 times; 2 ch, sk 2 dc, 1 dc into next dc; 2 dc, sk 2 ch (1 dc into next dc) 4 times; 2 ch, sk 2 ch (1 dc into next ch) 3 times; 3 ch, (3 dc, 1 ch, 1 dc) into 1 ch lp; 4 ch, 1 sc into center of 5 ch lps of previous 2 rows (*bow made*); 4 ch, (1 dc into next dc) 3 times; 4 ch, 1 sc into center of 5 ch lps of previous 2 rows (2nd *bow made*); 4 ch, (1 dc into next dc) 7 times; turn.

Row 8. 3 ch (count as a dc); (1 dc into next dc) 6 times; 5 ch, 1 dc, sk bow, (1 dc into next dc) 3 times; 5 ch, sk bow; (3 dc, 1 ch, 1 dc) into 1 ch lp; 3 ch, sk 3 dc, (1 dc into next dc) 3 times; 2 ch, sk 2 ch, 1 dc into next dc, 2 ch, sk 2 dc, 1 dc into next dc; (2 dc into 2 ch lp, 1 dc into next dc) twice; 2 ch, sk 2 dc, 1 dc into next dc; (2 ch, sk 2 ch, 1 dc into next dc) 3 times; 2 ch, sk 2 dc, (1 dc into next dc) 4 times; 2 dc into 2 ch lp, 1 dc into next dc; 2 ch (1 dc into next dc) 7 times; turn.

Row 9. 9 ch; 1 dc into 5th ch from hook; (1 dc into next dc) 4 times; 1 dc into next dc; (2 ch, sk 2 dc, 1 dc into next dc) twice; 2 dc into 2 ch lp, (1 dc into next dc) 4 times; 2 ch, sk 2 dc, 1 dc into next dc;

(2 ch, sk 2 ch, 1 dc into next dc) twice; (2 ch, sk 2 dc, 1 dc into next dc) twice; 2 ch, sk 2 ch, 1 dc into next dc; 2 ch, sk 2 ch, (1 dc into next dc) 3 times; 3 ch; 3 dc, 1 ch, 1 dc into 1 ch lp; 5 ch, sk 3 dc and 5 ch lp; (1 dc into next dc) 3 times; 5 ch, sk 5 ch, (1 dc into next dc) 7 times; turn.

Row 10. 3 ch (count as a dc); (1 dc into next dc) 6 times; 4 ch, 1 sc into center of 5 ch of previous 2 rows (*bow made*); 4 ch, (1 dc into next dc) 3 times; 4 ch, 1 sc into center of 5 ch of previous 2 rows (2nd *bow made*); 4 ch, (3 dc, 1 ch, 1 dc) into 1 ch lp; 3 ch (1 dc into next dc) 3 times; (2 ch, sk 2 ch, 1 dc) 4 times; (1 dc into next dc) 6 times; (2 ch, sk 2 ch, 1 dc into next dc) 4 times; 1 dc into next dc; (2 ch, sk 2 ch, 1 dc into next dc) twice; (1 dc into next dc) twice; turn.

Row 11. Sl st into next 7 dc; (2 dc into 2 ch lp, 1 dc into next dc) twice; 2 ch, sk 2 dc; (1 dc into next dc) 4 times; 2 dc into next 2 dc lp, 1 dc into next dc; (2 ch, sk 2 ch, 1 dc into next dc) 5 times; (2 dc into 2 ch lp, 1 dc into next dc) twice; (2 ch, sk 2 ch lp, 1 dc into next dc) twice; (1 dc into next dc) twice; 3 ch, (3 dc, 1 ch, 1 dc) into 1 ch lp; 5 ch, sk bow, (1 dc into next dc) 3 times; 5 ch, sk bow, (1 dc into next dc) 7 times; turn.

Row 12. 3 ch (count as a dc); (1 dc into next dc) 6 times; 5 ch, sk 5 ch, (1 dc into next dc) 3 times; 5 ch, sk 5 ch, (3 dc, 1 ch, 1 dc) into 1 ch lp; 3 ch, (1 dc into next dc) 3 times; 2 ch, sk 2 ch lp, 1 dc into next dc; 2 dc into 2 ch lp, 1 dc into next dc; (2 ch, sk 2 dc, 1 dc into next dc) twice; 2 dc into 2 ch lp, 1 dc into next dc; (2 ch, 1 dc into next dc) twice; 2 dc into 2 ch lp; (1 dc into next dc) 4 times; (2 ch, sk 2 dc, 1 dc into next dc) twice; (1 dc into next dc) 6 times; turn.

Row 13. Sl st into next 7 dc; 3 ch (count as a dc); (2 dc into 2 ch lp, 1 dc into next dc) twice; 2 ch, sk 2 dc, (1 dc into next dc) 4 times; 2 dc into 2 ch lp, 1 dc into next dc; (2 ch, 1 dc into next dc) twice; (1 dc into next dc) 3 times; 2 dc into 2 ch lp; 1 dc into next dc; 2 ch, sk 2 ch lp, (1 dc into next dc) 4 times; 2 ch, sk 2 ch lp, (1 dc into next dc) 3 times; 3 ch; (3 dc, 1 ch, 1 dc) into 1 ch lp; 4 ch, 1 sc into center of 5 ch of previous 2 rows (*bow made*); 4 ch, (1 dc into next dc) 3 times; 4 ch, 1 sc into center of 5 ch of previous 2 rows (2nd *bow made*); 4 ch (1 dc into next dc) 7 times; turn.

Row 14. 3 ch (count as a dc); (1 dc into next dc) 6 times; 5 ch, sk bow, (1 dc into next dc) 3 times;

5 ch, sk bow, (3 dc, 1 ch, 1 dc) into 1 ch lp; 3 ch (1 dc into next dc) 3 times; 2 ch, (1 dc into next dc) 4 times; (2 ch, 1 dc into next dc) 4 times; 2 dc into 2 ch lp, (1 dc into next dc) 4 times; 2 ch, sk 2 dc, 1 dc into next dc; 2 ch, sk 2 ch, (1 dc into next dc) 7 times; turn.

Row 15. Sl st into next 7 dc; 3 ch (count as a dc); (2 dc into 2 ch lp, 1 dc into next dc) twice; 2 ch, sk 2 dc, (1 dc into next dc) 4 times; 2 dc into 2 ch lp, 1 dc into next dc; 2 ch, sk 2 ch, (1 dc into next dc) twice; 2 dc into 2 ch lp; (1 dc into next dc) 4 times; 2 ch, sk 2 dc, (1 dc into next dc) 3 times; 3 ch; (3 dc, 1 ch, 1 dc) into 1 ch lp; 5 ch, sk 3 dc and 5 ch lp, (1 dc into next dc) 3 times; 5 ch, sk 5 ch, (1 dc into next dc) 7 times; turn.

Row 16. 3 ch (count as a dc); (1 dc into next dc) 6 times; 4 ch, 1 sc into center of 5 ch of previous 2 rows (*bow made*); 4 ch, (1 dc into next dc) 3 times; 4 ch, 1 sc into center of 5 ch of previous 2 rows (2nd *bow made*); 4 ch (3 dc, 1 ch, 1 dc) into 1 ch lp; 3 ch (1 dc into next dc) 3 times; 2 ch, sk 2 ch, 1 dc into next dc; 2 ch, sk 2 dc, (1 dc into next dc) 4 times;

(2 dc into 2 ch lp, 1 dc into next dc) twice; (1 dc into next dc) 3 times; 2 ch, sk 2 dc, 1 dc into next dc; 2 ch, sk 2 ch, (1 dc into next dc) 7 times; turn.

Row 17. Sl st into next 7 dc; 3 ch (count as a dc); (2 dc into 2 ch lp, 1 dc into next dc) twice; (2 ch, sk 2 dc, 1 dc into next dc) 4 times; (2 ch, sk 2 ch, 1 dc into next dc) twice; (1 dc into next dc) twice; 3 ch, (3 dc, 1 ch, 1 dc) into 1 ch lp; 5 ch, sk 3 dc and bow, (1 dc into next dc) 3 times; 5 ch, sk bow, (1 dc into next dc) 7 times; turn.

Row 18. 3 ch (count as a dc); (1 dc into next dc) 6 times; 5 ch, sk 5 ch, (1 dc into next dc) 3 times; 5 ch, sk 5 ch, (3 dc, 1 ch, 1 dc) into 1 ch lp; 3 ch, sk 3 dc and 3 ch lp, (1 dc into next dc) 3 times; (2 ch, 1 dc into next dc) 6 times; (1 dc into next dc) 6 times.

Keeping bow pattern correct*, repeat Rows 3–8 inclusive until work is the length required.

* Note: The bow pattern on the straight edge of shelf edging takes 3 rows for a pattern repeat whereas the peaked edge uses 17 rows for each pattern repeat. Consequently, the *bow made* row will not fall on the same rows as before.

A typical Victorian kitchen showing an antique Crocheted Shelf Liner.

Weathered Hat Box

For the Box:
large wooden hat box
fine sandpaper
cloth
wood sealer
medium size paintbrush
acrylic paints—gold or brown and cream
crackle medium
1 large transparent floral decal (available from ceramic suppliers)
5 medium-size transparent floral decals
large water container
antiquing patina (optional)
matte spray varnish

For the Lining (optional):
thick cardboard, pencil
scissors, pins, tape measure
polyester batting (wadding)
spray adhesive
1 generous yard (1 m) velvet fabric
quick-drying craft glue
gold braid

Sand the outside of the hat box (including the lid) with the fine sandpaper and wipe over the box with a cloth. Apply sealer and then a base coat of either the gold or the brown paint—two coats should be enough for a good cover. Set aside.

Weathered Hat Boxes. The front hat box has been painted with an antique finish.

When paint is dry, brush on one smooth, even coat of crackle medium over the base coat. Be sure not to apply the coat too thickly or it will run. Let it set for 20 minutes to one hour, then carefully brush on the cream paint in quick, even brush strokes. The size of the cracks will depend on the thickness of the paint; *i.e.* thin paint will produce fine cracks and thick paint will produce large cracks. Vary the thickness over the box for effect but never brush back over the paint after you have applied it.

Note: The composition of acrylic paint varies from brand to brand. Some paints may not crackle as desired. For the best results, make a small test piece first.

Leave the box to dry for at least 24 hours before applying the decals.

Immerse the large floral transparent decal in the large water container until the decal slides off of the backing paper. Position the decal (tacky side down) on the lid of the box and carefully smooth out the bubbles with the soft clean cloth. If there are any bubbles remaining after the decal dries, carefully prick these with a pin.

Apply the five medium-size floral decals evenly around the outside of the box in the same manner.

As an option, antique the box using the antiquing medium. Spray with matte varnish to complete.

Lining the Hat Box

Place the box on the thick cardboard and carefully draw around the outside edge of the box. Cut out the circle approximately 3/16 in. (5 mm) in from the pencil line. (Test-fit the cardboard circle on the inside bottom of the box—you may have to trim the edges a little more to fit inside the box with enough space to allow for the fabric to turn under.) Spray adhesive onto the cardboard circle, lay it down on the batting (wadding) and trim back the edges.

Cut a piece of velvet fabric 1⅛ in. (3 cm) larger than the cardboard and lightly spray-glue to the batting (wadding) side of the circle. Cut slits about ¾ in. (19 mm) apart into the edge of the fabric around the circle. Use craft glue to attach this edge to the cardboard. Be sure not to buckle the cardboard by pulling the fabric too tight.

Measure and cut a strip of batting (wadding) for the inside of the box, as follows: to cover the inside of the box, measure the circumference around the top and add 1⅝ in. (4 cm). Glue the batting (wadding) in place. To obtain the measurements for the strip of fabric to line the box after padding, measure from the top edge to the bottom and add 1⅝ in. (4 cm). If possible cut the fabric with a selvage on one long edge; fold back one of the ends and glue ⅜ in. (10 mm) to prepare a finished edge.

Work on a small section of the box at a time, applying glue around the inside top edge and then attaching one long edge of the fabric. Repeat this until you have lined the entire box; overlap the finished-off edge and complete by running a line of glue down the underneath side of the overlapped fabric and sticking it down. Glue the loose fabric from the sides to the bottom of the box, then carefully insert the cardboard circle to the bottom of the box.

Glue the gold braid around the top edge of the box, covering the edge of the fabric. Line the inside lid in the same way but use batting (wadding) only on the cardboard circle not the sides. You may need to use a finer braid on the edge for the lid to fit.

Close-up of the antique weathered Hat Box.

Lampshades

Choosing the Frame

Frames for lampshades vary considerably in size and shape. When choosing a frame, take the lamp base into the shop where you except to find the right shape. You can also look for a second-hand frame and remove the old covering.

Always remember that it is no more difficult to do a complicated shape than it is to do a very basic shape. Victorian shapes have a distinctive look of curves and scallops.

Getting Started

All metallic parts of the frame should be bound before a cover is added. Before commencing the binding, clean the frame of any welding material, rust, old bindings if this is a re-used or antique shade frame. Do this by using a piece of steel wool and wiping over the frame until it is completely clean. Then make a pattern of the shape: place the frame on a piece of paper and draw around the inside of the different-shaped panels with a pencil—one pattern for each distinct shape.

Binding the Frame

To bind the wire frame, use either sewing tape or bias binding. Follow the rule that always applies to binding: measure the length of the article to be bound and double it for the amount of tape needed. Measure and double the length of the top and bottom rings and of every rib (or strut).

Glue one measured length of tape to the bottom ring at the base of each wire upright. It is then a matter of wrapping the tape around that rib, overlapping slightly and pulling reasonably tight to keep the tape from slipping. Finish by gluing the tape to the top ring. Repeat for each rib.

Glue the tape you cut for the bottom ring to any part of the wire and begin binding. As you arrive at a rib, bind the tape around it in a figure eight; then carry on to the next upright and repeat the process, as illustrated in diagram 1. Finish by gluing the tail to the beginning of the wrap.

Do the top ring in the same manner.

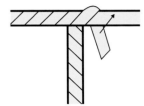

Diagram 1

The Fabric

When choosing the fabric for shades, take into consideration the amount of light you want to shine through it, any problems of cleaning and the difficulty in making.

Many dress materials and soft-furnishing fabrics are suitable—muslin, jersey, lace curtaining, cotton and velvet.

Using the pattern you drew before doing the binding, cut panels from the fabric, allowing an extra ¾ in. (19 mm) all around. Cut one piece for each section.

Gluing Panels

Using quick-drying craft glue on the outside binding of one rib only, rub the glue in until it is tacky and place the fabric panel over the section of the frame to be covered; rub until the fabric adheres adequately.

Repeat the process with every alternate section, until half of the frame is glued on one side only.

Returning to the first panel, repeat the same glue-applying process on the other rib and stretch the fabric tightly across the panel of the frame until it adheres securely. Do the same for the other panels, stretching each panel of fabric tight. Attach the fabric to the top and bottom rings in the same manner. When all alternate panels are completed, trim the fabric—using scissors—back to the edge of each upright; there must not be any fabric overlapping the ribs or showing on the inside of the frame.

Repeat the process on the other panels until all have all been covered.

Braiding

Run a line of glue down the frame over the raw edges of the fabric, then, starting at the top, place braid down onto the glue and press firmly onto the wire. Repeat until all raw edges are covered. Then glue more braid around the top.

Fringing

To obtain a two-tone color fringe for the shade, start with a desired base color, neatly roll the heading of the fringe into a large tassel—be careful to keep it level—and pin to hold. Prepare the desired dye. Under a slow-running tap, make a watermark half way up the fringe, making sure the top half remains completely dry.

Holding the fringe firmly, carefully dip it into the dye. It will fade out at the watermark. Lay the fringing out flat to dry. When the fringing is completely dry, attach it to the shade by gluing to the inside bottom ring of the frame.

Tassels

For one tassel, cut a 6 in. (15 cm) length of fringing, roll up and glue (diagram 2).

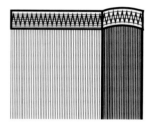

Diagram 2

Turn the tassel upside down and evenly spread the fringe over the glued end. Using a single strand of fringe tie a knot under the head, forming a tassel (diagram 3).

Diagram 3

Points to Remember

1. Tape all wires using bias binding with one side folded out, or sewing tape.

2. Always make a paper pattern—to obtain an exact shape—before binding the frame.

3. When gluing fabric to the frame, work alternate panels, allowing them to dry; the final panels are glued over the edge of the first panels.

4. Allow glue to become very tacky before applying fabric; otherwise glue soaks into fabric and adheres only with difficulty.

5. If you intend to color fringe in a fabric dye, always make the tassels first; roll the measured length of fringing into a large tassel and pin.

FLORAL LAMPSHADE

wire lampshade frame
steel wool
pencil, paper, scissors
bias binding or sewing tape
quick-drying craft glue
floral print fabric, dye
*trimmings—braid, fringing, nylon thread and pearls

Floral Lampshade.

* To ascertain the length required for the braid, measure all areas to be covered and add an extra 10 percent. For the fringing, measure the circumference of the bottom of the frame; purchase an extra 6 in. (15 cm) for each tassel you want.

Follow the general instructions for covering a lampshade.

Dye the fringing and attach it. To make the pearl loops, thread enough pearls onto a nylon thread to loop from the bottom of each small scallop. Attach a tassel to the center of the pearl loop. Stitch either end of the pearl loop to the lower edge of the covered frame.

CREAM BEADED LAMPSHADE

*wire lampshade, either double scalloped or
*empire shaped
scissors, pencil, paper, steel wool
bias binding or sewing tape
**satin fabric and lace in cream color
quick-drying craft glue
20 in. (50 cm) string
20 in. (50 cm) gathering cord
sewing machine, iron
braid for trimming
6 in. (15 cm) fringing
seed beads and bugle beads
clear nylon thread, beading needle*

* If empire shaped follow the previous instructions for covering the lampshade and the following instructions for decorating the lampshade.

** To figure how much satin fabric you need measure the circumference of the shade at its widest point and add 1⅝ in. (4 cm). Measure the height and add 2 in. (5 cm). The lace requirement depends on the size of the ovals to be covered.

To begin the lampshade follow the general instructions through binding the frame, but the only pattern to cut is for a lower oval. Now cut the satin oblong as described above. Join the two short edges of the satin with a ⅜ in. (10 mm) seam to form a cylinder. Hem the top edge by turning back ⅜ in. (10 mm) and pressing, and then turning back another ⅜ in. (10 mm) and sewing around ¼ in. (6 mm) from the

edge. Thread the gathering cord through the casing but do not gather yet.

Rub craft glue onto the bound frame at the bottom until it becomes sticky. Pull the fabric cylinder down onto the frame, as in diagram 4.

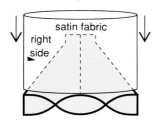

Diagram 4

Press the fabric onto the frame, gathering evenly where necessary to fit the scallop shapes. Trim the excess fabric back to the lower scallop shape. Tie the string around the top of the frame, over the fabric. Adjust the gathers evenly around the frame (diagram 5).

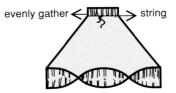

Diagram 5

Pull up the gathering cord in the top casing until the fabric is firm and evenly gathered. Stitch the cord to hold in position. Trim the excess fabric and neaten the casing to cover the cord. Leave the outer string in place for now.

Using the pattern already traced off the oval shape, cut the required pieces of lace, allowing an extra ⅜ in. (10 mm) all round.

Attach the lace following the general gluing instructions. Trim the excess lace.

Attach the braid by crossing in a figure eight (diagram 6) at the intersection of each oval and allow to dry.

When attaching the fringes leave 2¾ in. (7cm) hanging at the center of each scallop; pull the remaining fringe into a tassel below the junction of

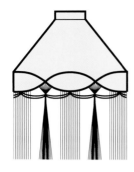

Diagram 6

Diagram 7

each scallop. Use a single strand of fringe to tie the tassel together.

Thread a variety of seed beads and bugle beads onto the clear nylon thread using a beading needle; knot the end and put aside.

Again thread the beading needle with nylon thread. Place a tiny stitch at each grouped tassel and at the center of each scallop, leaving 2⅜ in. (6 cm) tails hanging—this thread will be used to secure the strand of beads at these points.

Starting with the strand of beads to be looped around the lamp shade, tie at the beginning and secure at each point. Repeat this twice around the shade—see diagram 7. Then secure the strands that hang down over the tassel. Snip the nylon thread close to the knots.

Thread a strand of seed beads and bugle beads to go around the top ring of the shade. Remove the string that was holding the gathers. Wrap the string of beads around this section and secure with a knot.

The Cream Beaded Lampshade showing the bead work.

Candlewick Cushion

scissors, pins
1½ yd (1.4 m) white cotton fabric
tracing (graphite) paper
7 in. (18 cm) embroidery hoop
white candlewick thread
Size 22 chenille needle
dry towel
iron
1⅞ yd (1.7 m) of ³⁄₁₆ in. (5 mm) satin ribbon
2 yd (1.8 m) broderie beading
white sewing thread
sewing machine
tape measure
3½ yd (3.2 m) of 3⅛ in. (8 cm) wide broderie
lace edging
13¾ in. (35 cm) zipper
15¾ in. (40 cm) square cushion inner

Embroidery stitches used:
colonial knot

Cut out a 17 in. (43 cm) square of the white fabric. Trace the candlewicking design, and mirror-image the other side for a complete design, then transfer the design onto the fabric with tracing (graphite) paper.

Position the fabric in the embroidery hoop and use the white candlewick thread to embroider the design by stitching a colonial knot over every dot on the pattern.

After the embroidery is completed, wash the fabric in hot soapy water to shrink the embroidery. Rinse well, then roll in a clean dry towel and squeeze gently. Lay it face down on the ironing board and press. Thread the ribbon through the beading and stitch it to the front of the cushion 1⅛ in. (3 cm) in from the outside edges, making sure to mitre each of the corners (see diagram 1).

Trim edge of the cushion with a double frill, made up of the white fabric and the 3⅛ in. (8 cm) wide broderie lace edging.

To make the frill, first create a length of fabric 6⅞ in. x 4¾ yd (17 cm x 4.3 m) by cutting and joining together as many pieces as necessary to produce 4¾ yd (4.3 m).

Gather the 4¾ yd (4.3 m) length by stitching two rows along the raw edges with the machine set on a stitch length of 4.5. Gently pull up the threads until the ruffle measures the length of all four sides of the cushion together—1⅞ yd (1.7 m), plus a little more for easing at the corners. Gather the broderie lace edging to the same length.

To make the backing of the cushion, cut two rectangles of the white fabric 16 x 9 in. (40 x 23 cm) and sew these together with the zipper in between (as in diagram 2).

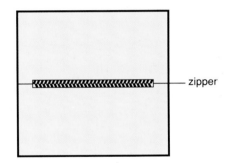

— zipper

Diagram 2

Sew all the pieces into a complete cushion by laying the back piece (unzip the zipper) face up on a flat surface, then arranging the frill, raw edges to raw edges, around the edges of the cushion; ease extra gathers into the corners so it sits well when turned out. Pin in place and then position the gathered lace in the same way over the frill (see diagram 3).

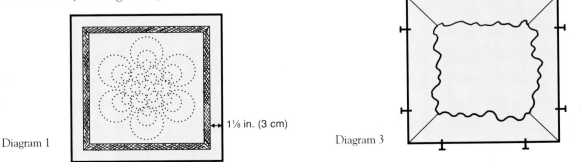

1⅛ in. (3 cm)

Diagram 1

Diagram 3

Lay the embroidered front of the cushion face down over the other layers, aligning the edges neatly. Carefully remove the pins from the first three layers and re-pin through all of the four layers.

Machine a ¼ in. (6 mm) seam around all of the sides; back-tack to secure stitching. Turn the pillow out through the open zipper and press.

Candlewicking is an age-old craft beautifully recreated with this white-on-white Candlewick Cushion.

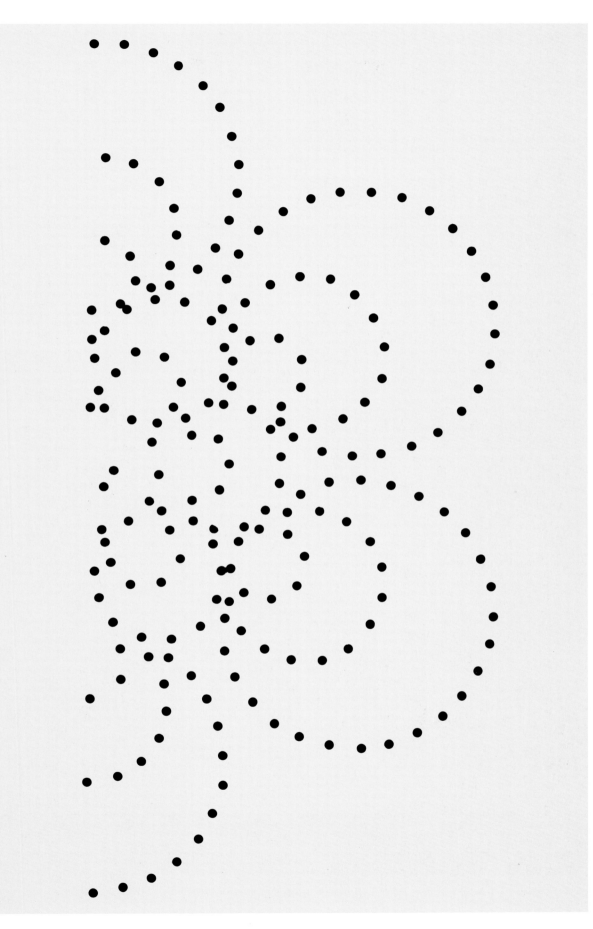

Victorian Cat Cushion

20 in. (50 cm) damask cloth with evenweave insert for
cross stitch
transfer pencil
DMC stranded threads: black, light rose, rose, green
No. 10 embroidery needle
white candlewick thread
No. 22 tapestry needle
20 in. (50 cm) lace edging
white sewing thread
sewing machine
polyester toy stuffing
scissors, pins
wooden skewer
iron

Embroidery stitches used:
cross stitch
chain stitch
satin stitch

Enlarge the scaled pattern as instructed on page 4. Position and pin the pattern over the damask so that the evenweave insert is centered on the cat's chest. Cut out two body pieces and two tail pieces. Transfer the embroidery design onto the front of the cat using the transfer pencil.

Using two strands of black floss, embroider the eyes and nose in satin stitch. Work the cross stitch according to the color legend. Stitch the other

Cats were popular pets during the Victorian era and were often reproduced in needlework and ceramics.

cat's face

cat's tail

cat's left ear

cat's rear end

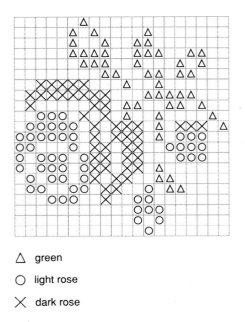

△ green

○ light rose

✕ dark rose

embroidery, following the stitch legend and using the white candlewick thread. Position the lace on the front of the cat and pin, then attach by top-stitching the header of the lace.

When the embroidery is complete, place the tail pieces right sides together and machine stitch around the entire shape, leaving the larger end of the tail open. Turn right side out and stuff firmly, using a skewer to push the stuffing into the corner. Baste across the end of the tail ¼ in. (6 mm) from the end. Pin the tail to the front body piece where marked, then lay the back over both, all right sides face to face, and pin all together. Sew around the entire shape, leaving a 4 in. (10 cm) opening at the bottom for turning right side out. Turn out and press. Stuff firmly and slip stitch the opening closed by hand.

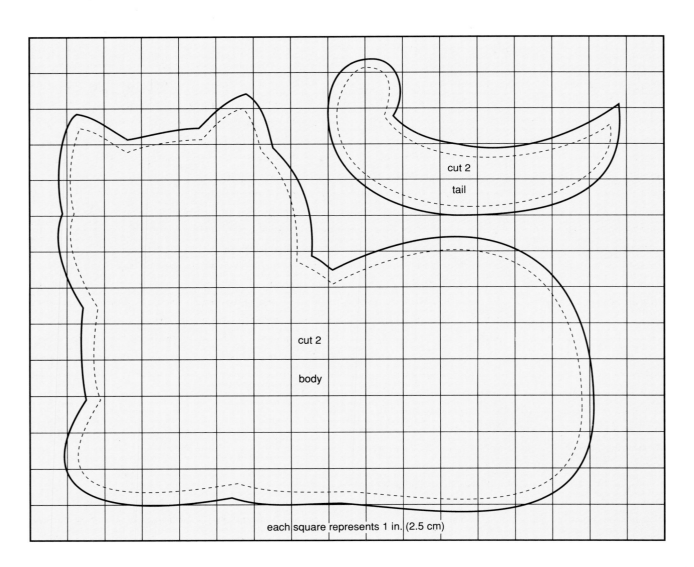

cut 2

tail

cut 2

body

each square represents 1 in. (2.5 cm)

Découpage

piece to be decorated
fine sandpaper
soft cloth
water-based sealer
soft-bristle brush
acrylic paint (optional)
suitable pictures (wrapping paper, scraps,
printed matter)
sharp-curved scissors (such as cuticle scissors)
water-based craft glue and brush
soft damp cloth
oil-based colored pencils
polyurethane varnish—gloss or matte
wet-and-dry sandpaper—grades 400, 600 and 1200
(medium, fine and ultrafine)
extremely fine steel wool
fine paste wax polish
muslin

Lightly sand the chosen piece and wipe over with a soft cloth. Apply one coat of sealer and then if necessary (if the surface is not to be completely covered with pictures) give the piece a basecoat of acrylic paint. You might like to apply another coat of sealer over the acrylic paint. If you are using a metal piece, be extra careful to remove all rust prior to sealing.

Before cutting out the pictures, use sealer on both sides of the paper. Depending on the image, you may need to apply two or three coats. Carefully cut out the pictures as accurately as possible, using the sharp-curved scissors: hold the scissors with the curved point facing outward and move the picture through the scissors to achieve a smooth, accurate finish.

Cut more pictures than necessary, so that you will have a large selection to choose from when designing your piece. When laying out your design, you may find it easier to draw the shape of your piece on paper and arrange the pictures on that before trying them on the actual piece. Try to overlap your pictures and to co-ordinate colors for a harmonious effect.

Apply a generous amount of the water-based craft glue to the piece to be decorated: never coat the picture because it would become soggy. Lay the picture in position then apply a small dab of glue to the top of the picture and rub it with your fingertips to spread it evenly. Make sure there are no air bubbles or excess glue under the picture by smoothing it out with a soft damp cloth. Do not press too hard, as this would not leave enough glue under the picture. Wipe over the picture to remove the glue from the top surface. Continue adding more pictures in the same way until your design is complete. Leave to dry.

To prepare your piece for varnishing, touch up the white edges and spots with oil-based colored pencils, smudging the pencil marks to blend in with the picture. Seal the entire piece before varnishing.

Always use a soft-bristle brush for varnishing. Never brush back and forth because this encourages air bubbles and remember to change the direction of your brush strokes with each coat of varnish. Apply very thin coats of varnish for the first few layers. If wrinkles appear, leave the piece for a few days before revarnishing. In any case, leave each coat to dry for at least 24 hours before applying the next one.

The aim of découpage finish is to attain a smooth, glasslike surface similar to that of lacquered furniture. To achieve this, after 20 coats of varnish sand the piece lightly to remove bumps and to even out crevices, using grade 400 wet-and-dry paper and sanding in one direction with a small amount of water. Apply 8 more coats of varnish, sanding with the grade 600 wet-and-dry before each coat. Use grade 1200 wet-and-dry for the next 2 coats. Apply a final layer to finish the varnishing.

Rub the extremely fine steel wool over the surface to remove the gloss; wipe clean before waxing. Apply the wax in small sections at a time, vigorously rubbing it in with the muslin for a silky smooth surface.

Because the varnish takes six months to cure, take extra care with your piece and wax it periodically for protection.

Overleaf: During the 19th century ladies of leisure collected fancy-paper scraps and applied them to various decorated pieces.

Topiary Tree

39 in. (1 m) length of branch approximately 1½ in. (4 cm) thick
8 in. (20 cm) ball of florist's Oasis
flowerpot, broken brick or gravel
plaster of Paris
3 bunches of dried hydrangeas
florist's wire
9 stems of silk leaves
gold spray paint
8 large silk roses—4 dark red, 4 dusty pink
8 medium silk roses—4 dark red, 4 dusty pink
26 silk rose buds—13 dark red, 13 dusty pink
24 stems of dried lavender
assorted dried flowers
silk and dried baby's breath (gypsophila)
small seedpods with long stems
8⅔ yd (8 m) of ⅛ in. (3 mm) satin ribbon
4⅓ yd (3.85 m) of ⅝ in. (16 mm) lace ribbon
2⅓ yd (2 m) of ⅛ in. (3 mm) gold pearl string
2½ yd (2.2 m) of 1 in. (2.5 cm) double-sided satin ribbon

scissors
quick-drying craft glue

Wedge the branch into the base of the Oasis ball deep enough to form a 2 in. (5 cm) indent. Remove the branch and cover the first 3 in. (7.5 cm) of the stick with quick-drying craft glue, then push the branch back into the ball at least 3 in. (7.5 cm).

To set the branch into a pot, place broken bricks or gravel around the base of the branch to hold it securely in the pot. Following the manufacturer's instructions, prepare the plaster of Paris and pour into the pot. Leave to set.

Break the bunches of hydrangeas into flowerettes approximately 2 in. (5 cm) in diameter and wire each one. Push the wired bunches into the Oasis ball until it is completely covered. Push in the silk leaves equally around the ball and lightly spray with gold paint.

Trim the stems of the roses so that they are long enough to push into the ball and still protrude 4 in. (10 cm) out from the hydrangeas. Push in the largest roses first, then the medium and then the buds in a balanced arrangement around the ball, varying the lengths of the stems so that some of the medium roses and the rose buds protrude more than others.

The hydrangeas and the roses form the bulk of the topiary tree. Push the remaining flowers and seed pods into the gaps to give an overall balanced look.

Cut eleven 13¾ in. (35 cm) lengths of the lace and the ⅛ in. (3 mm) satin ribbon. Hold one length of each together and fold a double figure-eight bow. Pinch together in the center to form a four-loop bow and wrap wire around the pinched center. Repeat with the other cut lengths. Push the loops in evenly around the ball.

Cut five 9¾ in. (25 cm) lengths of the gold pearl garland and fold each into two loops, wire the ends and push into the topiary ball.

Loop the remaining ⅛ in. (3 mm) satin ribbon and the 1 in. (2.5 cm) double-sided ribbon into bows and wire onto the branch at the base of the topiary ball. Loop the remaining gold pearl garland and attach it, too, with wire to the branch over the bows.

Topiary Tree complemented by the Hydrangea Swag.
Flowers were a focal point of the Victorian era.

Hydrangea Swag

hank of raffia 39 in. (1 m) in length and
approximately 4 in. (10 cm) in circumference
when bundled
3 large heads of dried hydrangeas
fine florist's wire
green Parafilm tape or florist's tape
6 cream dried straw flowers (helichrysum)
4⅓ yd (4 m) of ⅝ in. (16 mm) wide dusty pink
cut-edge ribbon
statice
6 small bunches of silk baby's breath (gypsophila)
4⅓ yd (4 m) of ⅝ in. (16 mm) wide cream
straight lace
5 dark red silk rose buds
5 dusty pink silk rose buds
6½ yd (6 m) of ⅝ in. (16 mm) wide
double-edged lace
quick-drying craft glue
2⅛ yd (2 m) of ¾ in. (19 mm) wide dusty pink
cut-edge ribbon
14 in. (36 cm) of 20-gauge florist's wire

Tie the raffia 8 in. (20 cm) in from one end with a single length of raffia. Hook the raffia over a doorknob and begin braiding (plaiting). Stop 8 in. (20 cm) from the other end and tie with another single length of raffia (see diagram 1).

Diagram 1

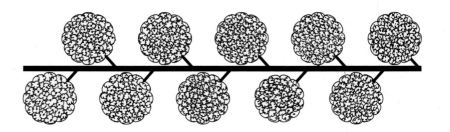

Diagram 3

Cut the hydrangeas into small flowerettes, leaving the stems 2⅜ in. (6 cm) long. Wire each one with florist's wire and cover with Parafilm or florist's tape. Cut all the stems of the dried flowers to measure 2⅜ in. (6 cm); wire and cover with Parafilm or tape. Fold and wire five ribbon loops of the ⅜ in. (10 mm) wide ribbon and five loops of the ⅝ in. (16 mm) lace ribbon (see diagram 2). Cover the wire with Parafilm or florist's tape.

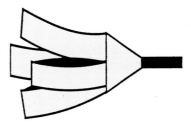

Diagram 2

Place the length of 20-gauge florist's wire on a flat surface and begin covering from one end, taping the hydrangea bunches on with the Parafilm (see diagram 3).

Arrange the silk rose buds in between the hydrangeas and secure them by their wire stems. Position the straw flowers and baby's breath (gypsophila) and attach in the same way. Attach the ribbon and lace loops, spread evenly among the flowers, and the same with the statice.

Run a thick line of glue down the center of the raffia braid and push the wire stem of the arrangement into the glue. Tie two large, full bows of the ¾ in. (19 mm) ribbon and glue onto each end over the tied ends of the braid.

$\mathscr{S}$mall $\mathscr{P}$rojects

"Fancy work" was a highly respected leisure activity for the ladies of the Victorian era. Embroidery was high on the list of desirable skills and a mark of refinement and taste. There was always a delightful collection of threads, fabrics, scissors, trinkets, braids and tassels, to be found spilling out of sewing baskets.

Pretty little items were made either as decorations for the home or as gifts for friends.

Above: Victorian Flowerpot complements lace curtains.
Opposite: The Embroidered Photo Frame is perfectly in keeping with the French writing desk with brass inlay (circa 1870) and black lacquer mother-of-pearl inlaid chair (circa 1875).

Scented Victorian Hat

cardboard circle 9⅞ in. (25 cm) in diameter

scissors

2 pieces of satin fabric each 12 in.-square
(30 x 30 cm)

quick-drying craft glue

39 in. (1 m) pregathered 3⅛ in. (8 cm)
wide edging lace

pins

20 in. (50 cm) of fine tulle

needle and thread

potpourri

39 in. (1 m) of ¾ in. (2 cm) wide cream
satin ribbon

20 in. (50 cm) open-weave lace

1⅝ yd (1.5 m) pearl string

scraps of pale-colored organza

florist's wire

2¾ yd (2.5 m) of 1 in. (2.5 cm) wide
insertion lace

assortment of silk flowers, leaves and greenery

Cut one piece of the satin fabric into a circle ¾ in. (19 mm) larger all around than the cardboard circle. Cut the other piece ³⁄₁₆ in. (5 mm) smaller than the cardboard circle. Smear a light layer of glue over one side of the cardboard circle and position it to adhere the larger piece of fabric with a ¾ in. (19 mm) overhang. Ease the overhanging fabric over to the other side of the cardboard and glue securely. Run a thin line of glue around the edge of the cardboard ⅜ in. (10 mm) in from the edge on this side. Glue the smaller circle of fabric over the turned raw edge of fabric.

Position the 3⅛ in. (8 cm) wide pregathered lace around the edge of the circle, covering the raw edge of the second circle of fabric and pin to hold in place. Glue it down.

Cut a piece of tulle 11 x 31½ in. (28 x 80 cm), then baste with a row of large tacking stitches down the center (as in diagram 1).

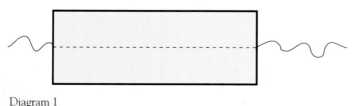

Diagram 1

Fold the tulle in half lengthwise along the gathering row and gently and firmly gather into a tight bunch in the center. This is the crown (see diagram 2). Coax the bottom edge into a circle approximately 8 in. (20 cm) in diameter.

Diagram 2

Smear a ¾ in. (19 mm) strip of glue around the satin-covered circle, 3⅛ in. (8 cm) from the edge. Push the crown onto the glue strip, leaving a small section unglued to poke the potpourri through. Fill the crown with potpourri and glue the tulle securely. Glue a band of the ¾ in. (19 mm) wide cream ribbon around the base of the crown. Fold the open-weave lace into a strip approximately 4 in. (10 cm) wide and drape around the crown of the hat, gently and softly twisting it as it goes around. Glue in place at intervals. Double the pearl string and drape around the brim, under and over the open-weave lace, leaving tails at the back to hang down.

Make three organza flowers by cutting the colored pieces of organza into squares 12 x 12 in. (30 x 30 cm), folding the fabric in half, gathering in to form a cabbage-rose shape and wiring the bases to secure the shape.

Fold a bow using two long tails from the insertion lace and glue this on one side of the hat. Cut two tails from the satin ribbon and glue these over the bow. Arrange the organza roses, silk flowers and greenery on top of the bow and glue in place.

Opposite: The Scented Victorian Hat is a simple project that will complement a Victorian bedroom.

Crocheted Edge Coat Hanger

wooden coat hanger
scissors, tape measure, iron, soft pencil
6 in. (15 cm) white cotton lawn
white cotton sewing thread, needle
polyester batting (wadding)
1 skein white embroidery floss
No. 7 sharp embroidery needle
DMC No. 60 white crochet cotton
No. 10 steel crochet hook (metric 1.00, English 5½)
10½ in. (26.5 cm) of ⅛ in. (3 mm) wide
white satin ribbon

Tension: 14 dc to 1 in. (2.5 cm)

Embroidery stitches used:
satin stitch

Cover the wire hook of the coat hanger by cutting a bias strip 1⅝ in. (4 cm) wide by 6 in. (15 cm) long. Press with an iron to take out all the stretch. Fold the fabric in half, right sides together, and stitch ³⁄₁₆ in. (5 mm) from the folded edge. Trim the seam allowance slightly narrower than the tube. Attach a double thread to the stitching and, using the eye of the needle, thread through the tubing to turn it right side out. Leave the thread attached as shown in diagram 1.

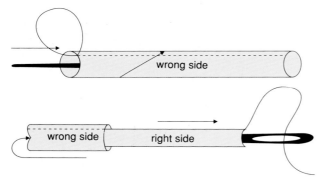

Diagram 1

Cover the hook and use the attached thread to turn under the raw ends of the tube and stitch. Cut a piece of batting (wadding) to fit around the wooden hanger and stitch in place, piercing a small hole through the batting (wadding) for the hook. Enlarge the pattern pieces following the instructions on page 127.

Cut out one piece of fabric using pattern piece No. 2. Fold the fabric in half lengthwise and make a ¼ in. (6 mm) buttonhole in the center on the fold line. Stitch along both ends but leave the bottom of the tube open (diagram 2). Turn right side out.

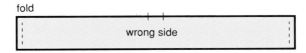

Diagram 2

Insert the coat hanger into the open side of the tube, working the covered hook carefully through the buttonhole. Turn in a ⅜ in. (10 mm) hem along the lower edge and slip stitch closed. Neatly hand sew the cover around the hook.

To make the embroidered cover cut two pieces of fabric according to pattern piece No. 1. Roll-and-whip the top and bottom edges. Lay one piece of the fabric over the embroidery pattern and, using the soft pencil, trace the pattern onto the center of the fabric. Use two strands of white embroidery floss to satin stitch the design.

With right sides together, join the two cover pieces along the top with a flat seam; leave an opening for the hook. Sew up the sides with a narrow French seam.

To make the crocheted edging, follow the instructions below.

Abbreviations and Symbols:
sh = shell (3 dc, 3 ch, 3 dc)
dc = double crochet
sk = skip
ch = chain
sl st = slip stitch
* An asterisk is used to mark the beginning of a portion of instructions that will be worked more than once.
() Parentheses are used to enclose instructions that should be worked the exact number of times specified after the parentheses.

Row 1. Make 15 ch and work (3 dc into the 8th ch from the hook; 3 ch 3 dc into next ch) *shell made*; (2 ch, sk 2 ch, 1 dc into next ch) twice. Turn.

From top: Heirloom Coat Hanger, Brazilian Embroidered Coat Hanger and Crocheted Edge Coat Hanger.

Row 2. 5 ch, (1 dc into next dc, 2 ch) twice; 1 sh into sh; 2 ch, sk 2 ch. Turn. 1 dc into next ch. Turn.

Row 3. 6 ch; 1 sh into sh; 2 ch, 2 dc into last dc of previous sk; (2 ch, 1 dc into next dc) twice; 2 ch, 1 dc into 3rd ch of 5 ch. Turn.

Row 4. 5 ch; (1 dc into next dc 2 ch) 4 times; 2 ch, 1 sh into sh; 2 ch, sk 2 ch, 1 dc into next ch. Turn.

Row 5. 6 ch; 1 sh into sh; 2 ch, 1 dc into last dc of previous sh; (2 ch, 1 dc into next dc) 4 times; 2 ch, 1 dc into 3rd chain of 5 ch. Turn.

Row 6. 5 ch; 1 dc into next dc; (2 ch, 1 dc into next dc) 5 times; 2 ch, 1 sh into sh; 2 ch, sk 2 ch, 1 dc into next ch. Turn.

Row 7. 6 ch; 1 sh into sh; 2 ch, 1 dc into last dc of previous sh; (2 ch, 1 dc into next dc) 6 times; 2 ch, 1 dc into 3rd of 5 ch. Turn.

Row 8. 5 ch, 1 dc into next dc; (2 ch, 1 dc into next dc) 7 times; 2 ch, 1 sh into sh; 2 ch, sk 2 ch, 1 dc into next ch. Turn.

Row 9. 6 ch; 1 sh into sh; 2 ch, 1 dc into last dc of previous sh; 2 ch, 1 dc. Turn.

Repeat Rows 2–9 inclusive 16 times and Rows 2–8 inclusive once.

Join work to form a circle by folding work in half and then sl st the beginning to the end.

Final Round. Sl st into square loop *(1 sc, 3 ch, 1 sc) 7 times; into peak work (1 sc, 3 ch, 1 sc, 3 ch, 1 sc); (1 sc, 3 ch, 1 sc) 7 times*. Repeat from * to * to end of round. Finish off thread.

Whip stitch the crocheted edging to the lower edge of the embroidered coat hanger cover. To complete, place the cover over the hanger and tie a satin ribbon bow around the base of the hook.

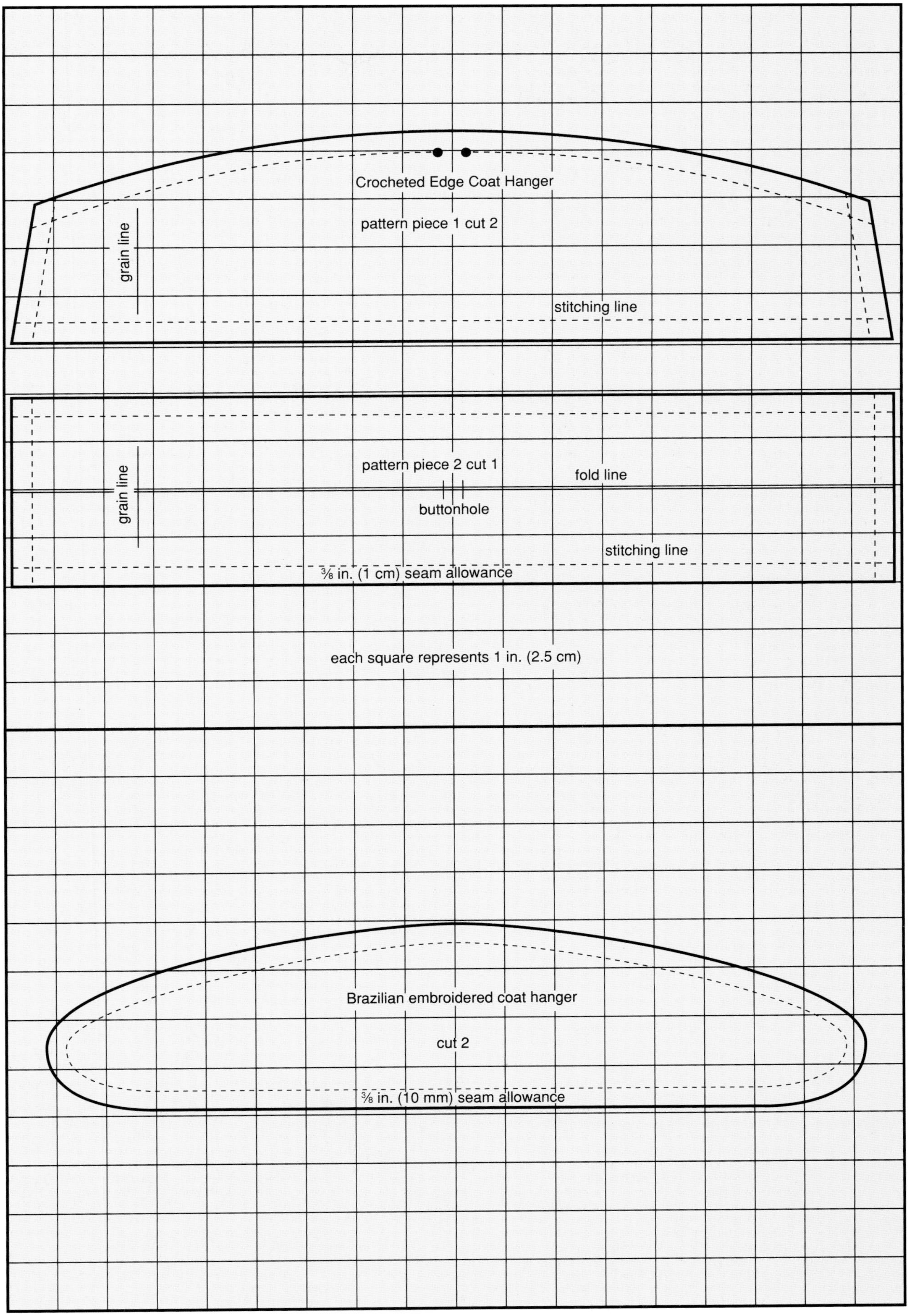

Crocheted Edge Coat Hanger

pattern piece 1 cut 2

grain line

stitching line

pattern piece 2 cut 1

fold line

grain line

buttonhole

stitching line

⅜ in. (1 cm) seam allowance

each square represents 1 in. (2.5 cm)

Brazilian embroidered coat hanger

cut 2

⅜ in. (10 mm) seam allowance

Brazilian Embroidered Coat Hanger

10 in. (25 cm) ivory raw silk
tracing (graphite) paper, pencil
ivory stranded embroidery floss
20 ivory "seed pearls"
No. 8 and No. 10 crewel embroidery needles
ivory sewing thread
2 strips of polyester batting (wadding), each
17 x 4 in. (43 x 10 cm)
scissors, pins
sewing machine, wooden coat hanger, iron
8 in. (20 cm) of 1/8 in. (3 mm) wide ivory
double-sided satin ribbon
loop turner
10 in. (25 cm) of 1/8 in. (3 mm) wide ivory satin
ribbon

Embroidery stitches used:
   bullion stitch
   couching stitch
   pistol stitch

Enlarge the scaled pattern on page 127 and cut two pieces of the raw silk. Use the tracing (graphite) paper to transfer the embroidery design to the center of the front cover piece.

The embroidery is worked with a single strand of floss and the No. 8 crewel embroidery needle. The seed pearls are added afterwards.

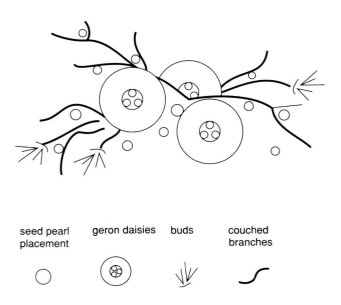

seed pearl   geron daisies   buds   couched
placement   branches

Embroidering the Design

To stitch the embroidery, make the geron daisies first. Work the petals in pistol stitch, with four wraps at the end of each stitch. Come up at the edge of the inner circle, wrap the needle 4 times, go down at the edge of the outer circle. The stitch should be approximately 5/16 in. (8 mm) long. Vary the length of each stitch slightly to make the petals different lengths. Give each of the buds 5 to 8 pistol stitches, and the calyx a 12 to 15 wrap bullion stitch.

Use the No. 10 crewel embroidery needle to fill the center of the daisies with three seed pearls. The half-flower gets only two pearls. Stitch the other beads as indicated. Use couching stitch for the branches.

Finishing

Cut two pieces of batting (wadding) to the size indicated by the stitching line on the enlarged pattern piece and stitch them together across the top, leaving a hole for the hook. Position over the hanger and sew the lower opening closed.

Place the embroidered front cover piece and back piece right sides together and stitch as shown in diagram 1. Turn right side out.

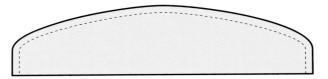

Diagram 1

Place the cover over the batting-covered coat hanger. Turn under a 5/8 in. (16 mm) seam across the lower edge and slip stitch the back and front together.

Cut a bias strip 1 1/8 x 5 7/8 in. (3 x 15cm) and iron, stretching it until there is no stretch left. Fold, the strip in half lengthwise and press. Stitch a 3/16 in. (5 mm) seam along the length of the bias strip, trim and neaten with a zigzag stitch (or overlock). Turn right side out with a loop turner. Place the tubular piece of fabric over the hook of the hanger, then stitch in place at the base. Trim the top end to size, turn in the raw edge and stitch to finish. Tie a small bow at the base of the hook.

Heirloom Coat Hanger

2⅛ yd (2 m) of 1⅝ in. (4 cm) wide lace insertion
34 in. (85 cm) of ⅟₁₆ in. (2 mm) entredeux
tape measure, scissors
No. 10 crewel embroidery needle
No. 5 cotton thread
strip of polyester batting (wadding)
wooden coat hanger
6 x 1⅛ in. (15 x 3 cm) cotton fabric—
cut on the bias
iron, sewing machine
loop turner
39 in. (1 m) of 1½ in. (3.8 cm) wide lace edging
pins
20 in. (50 cm) of ⅛ in. (3 mm) wide silk ribbon

Cut the lace insertion in half. Gather the lace by picking up one of the horizontal threads in the straight reinforced header gently pulling to approximately 17 in. (43 cm) in length. If the lace does not have this edge, hand- or machine-sew a small running stitch to gather it. The lace will need to be gathered on both sides (as shown in diagram 1).

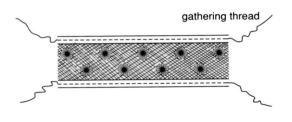

gathering thread

Diagram 1

Cut two pieces of the entredeux to the finished length of the coat hanger (allow for padding) and trim one side of each piece (diagram 2).

Diagram 2

Place the right sides together and whip stitch the entredeux to each side of one length of the gathered lace (see diagram 3).

Trim the other side of one of the entredeux and with right sides together, whip stitch the remaining piece of gathered lace insertion to the trimmed edge, leaving a small hole in the center (for the hanger's hook).

Diagram 3

Cover the hanger by wrapping strips of the batting (wadding) around the wood, starting at one end and overlapping each wrap just a little. Make sure to pad each end. Stitch the batting (wadding) to secure, especially around the hook.

Gently position the lace piece over the coat hanger, easing the hook through the hole in the top. Turn in the raw edges at each end and whip stitch.

Iron the bias strip, stretching as you go until there is no more stretch left, then fold the strip in half and press. Stitch a ³⁄₁₆ in. (5 mm) seam along the length of the strip, trim and neaten with a zigzag stitch (or overlock). With a loop turner, turn right side out. Place this bias tube over the hook and stitch in place at the base. Trim and turn in the other end and stitch closed.

Trim the entredeux on both lower edges of the lace cover. Whip stitch the two edges together the length of the hanger.

To complete the trimming, gather the lace edging to the finished length of the hanger, using the same method described for the lace insertion, and whip stitch it to the bottom edge.

Tie silk ribbon bows at the base of the hook.

Gift Soap Box

thin cardboard
fabric or wrapping paper
scissors
quick-drying craft glue
ruler
pencil
pretty soap
30 in. (75 cm) of narrow gold ribbon
small dried flowers

Trace the pattern onto paper and transfer to the cardboard, making sure to draw in all the lines on the pattern. Cut around the outside lines and glue this to the fabric or paper.

Carefully trim the fabric back to the edge of the cardboard and very lightly paint the edges with craft glue to stop the fabric from fraying.

Score the six pencilled lines with the sharp point of your scissors and fold the pasteboard in to form a box shape, folding the small flap piece over the back.

Tie the ribbon around the center of the box with a bow in the middle of the front, and decorate with small flowers.

To insert the soap, open the flap at one end.

The Gift Soap Box—a simple project to make for gift-giving.

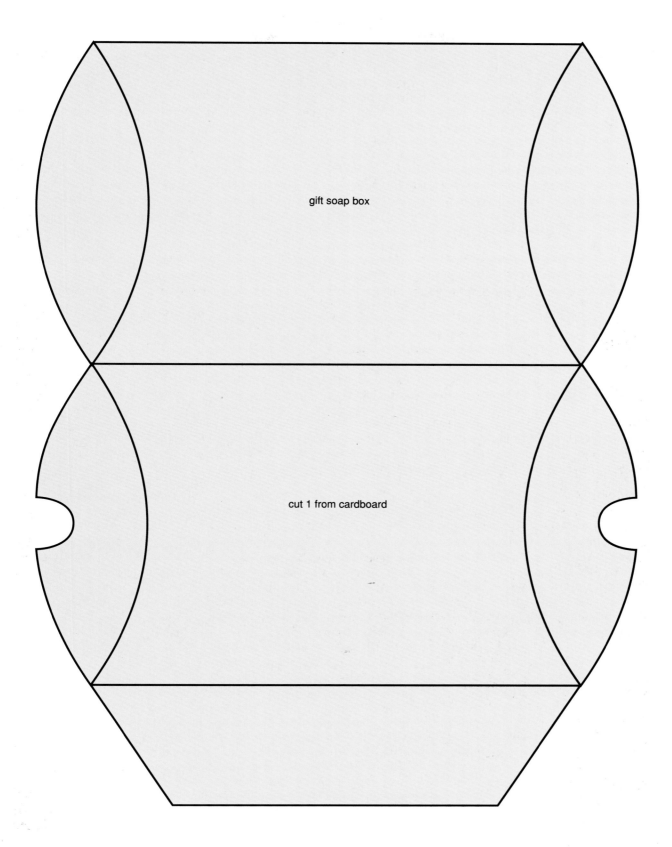

gift soap box

cut 1 from cardboard

Embroidered Photo Frame

*12 in. (30.5) of 45 in. (114 cm) wide water wave
taffeta (moiré taffeta)
basting thread and needle, pins, paper
tracing (graphite) paper
embroidery hoop, thick white cardboard
stranded embroidery floss in the same color
as the fabric used
No. 7 milliner's/straw needle
No. 8 crewel embroidery needle
craft knife, spray adhesive
polyester batting (wadding)
quick-drying craft glue, scissors
20 in. (50 cm) of silk cord
5 in. (13 cm) of ⅛ in. (3 mm) ribbon
sewing thread, soft lead pencil*

Embroidery stitches used:
    bullion knot stitch
    straight stitch
    French knot
    couching stitch

Trace the pattern for the photograph frame onto the paper. Position the paper on the back of the fabric, pin in place, and using a tacking stitch, baste around the drawn lines; tear away the paper. This will indicate the shape of the frame without the need to mark the fabric.

Trace the design for the embroidery, then transfer it onto the fabric with tracing (graphite) paper. Place the fabric in the embroidery hoop and embroider the design, following the legend on the pattern and the diagrams below.

Rolled Rosebud

Make two bullion knot stitches side by side, each approximately ¼ in. (6 mm) in length with 10–12 wraps. Across the base add a calyx with 12–14 wraps. Refer to diagram 1 for stitch placement.

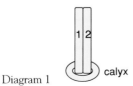

Diagram 1

Rolled Rose

Using two strands of embroidery floss and the No. 7 milliner's/straw needle, follow the steps in diagram 2. diagram 2.

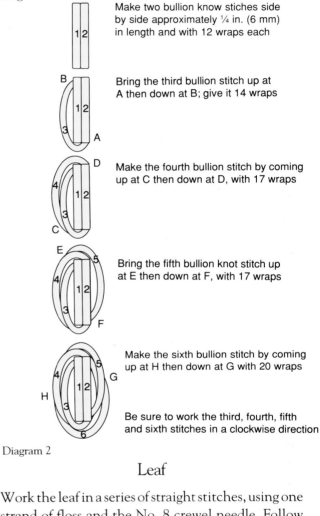

Make two bullion know stiches side by side approximately ¼ in. (6 mm) in length and with 12 wraps each

Bring the third bullion stitch up at A then down at B; give it 14 wraps

Make the fourth bullion stitch by coming up at C then down at D, with 17 wraps

Bring the fifth bullion knot stitch up at E then down at F, with 17 wraps

Make the sixth bullion stitch by coming up at H then down at G with 20 wraps

Be sure to work the third, fourth, fifth and sixth stitches in a clockwise direction

Diagram 2

Leaf

Work the leaf in a series of straight stitches, using one strand of floss and the No. 8 crewel needle. Follow diagram 3 to stitch.

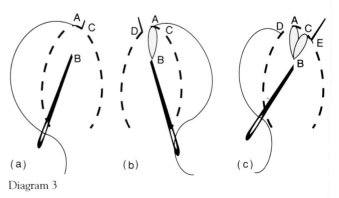

(a)   (b)   (c)

Diagram 3

The Embroidered Photo Frame is shown here with a close-up of a French writing desk.

Bring the thread up at A, pull the thread all the way through. Take the needle down at B and come up at C. Pull the thread all the way through (a).

Next take the needle down at B and come up at D. Pull the thread all the way through (b). Then for the third stitch, take the needle down at B again and come up at E (c). From then on, graduate the stitches down the leaf. Make sure you work from one side to the other, as shown in diagram 4.

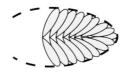

Diagram 4

Couched Branches

"Couching" means laying the thread on top of the fabric and catching it with an over stitch every now and again to hold it in the desired position, as instructed in the stitch glossary. Use only one strand of floss and work all the branches.

French Knots

Using one strand of floss, work all the French knots where indicated on the pattern.

Making the Frame

When the embroidery is complete, trace the patterns for the frame and the stand and transfer them to cardboard. To make the frame you will need three frame pieces (one with the center cut out) and two stand pieces; use a craft knife to cut them neatly.

Use spray adhesive to cover one side of the frame's front piece (the one with the cut-out center) with batting (wadding); trim back all the edges.

Lay the batting (wadding) side of the frame down on the back of the embroidery along the basted stitch lines. Trim back the fabric to allow ¾ in. (19 mm) beyond the outer edges. Apply craft glue around the outer edge of the frame, then wrap the fabric allowance over so that it adheres. For the picture opening stab a hole through the center of the fabric with the sharp point of the scissors; trim the fabric to leave a 1⅛ in. (3 cm) allowance. Snip the fabric at ¾ in. (19 mm) intervals (diagram 5). Pull the fabric tight and glue onto the cardboard. Remove the tacking stitches.

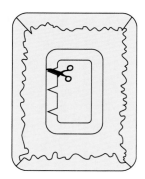

Diagram 5

Neatly glue the silk cord on the inside edge of the cut-out central picture opening.

Cut fabric for the two back pieces, leaving a ¾ in. (19 mm) allowance around all edges. Spray-glue the fabric to one side of each piece; glue the edges over onto the cardboard side on each piece.

Cut out fabric for the two stand pieces 1⅛ in. (3 cm) larger around all edges. Use spray adhesive to glue the cardboard stand pieces onto the fabric; fold over and glue the sides and the bottoms of both pieces as shown in diagram 6, leaving the top flaps.

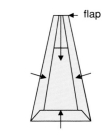

Diagram 6

Pierce a hole in the center of one stand; thread the ⅛ in. (3 mm) ribbon through the hole and knot on the reverse (cardboard) side. Coat the reverse sides of each stand with craft glue and stick together, including the fabric flaps at the top.

Place the bottom edge of the stand in line with the center base of one of the back pieces (fabric side) and draw a line the width of the top edge of the stand, excluding the top flap (diagram 7).

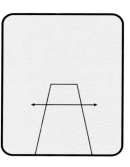

Diagram 7

Carefully slice along the line with the craft knife, cutting to the exact width all the way through the fabric and the cardboard. With the ribbon side of the stand facing the back piece, slide the fabric flap through the cut.

Turn over to the cardboard side and glue the loose flap down. Pierce another hole in the back piece, halfway between the base and the top of the stand, thread the ribbon through and knot.

Apply the glue to the cardboard sides of both back pieces and carefully glue them together. Apply glue to the cardboard side of the front piece, leaving one side free of glue so a photograph can be inserted, and press firmly onto the back pieces.

stand pattern

cut 2 from cardboard

● French knot   ◌ rolled rose   ⬮ rolled rosebud   🍃 leaf   branches

Crocheted Milk Jug Cover

compass
pencil
6 x 6 in. (15 x 15cm) piece of fine linen or lawn
scissors
cotton thread and needle for hemming
No. 8 sharp embroidery needle
size 10 steel crochet hook (metric 1.00, English 5½)
1 ball of DMC No. 60 white crochet cotton
12 glass beads

Tension = 18 dc to 1 in. (2.5 cm)

Abbreviations and Symbols:

dc = double crochet

sc = single crochet

sk = skip

ch(s) = chain(s)

sl st = slip stitch

lp(s) = loop(s)

rept = repeat

pc = picot (3 ch, sl st into first ch)

tr = treble

y.o.h = yarn over hook

fan = 5 dc worked into 1 dc

rnd = round

dle acorn = double acorn: (y.o.h and insert into 1st dc; draw through 2 lps leaving 2 lps on hook) rept twice; y.o.h insert into 4th dc; draw yarn through all 5 lps.

tr acorn = treble acorn: (y.o.h twice; draw yarn through 2 lps twice, leaving 2 lps on hook) 3 times; y.o.h twice; draw yarn through 2 lps then through all 5 remaining lps.

*An asterisk is used to mark the beginning and end of a portion of instructions that will be worked more than once.

() Parentheses are used to enclose instructions that should be worked the exact number of times specified after the parentheses.

Working the Pattern

Lightly draw on the fabric a circle 4½ in. (11.5 cm) in diameter and cut out. Roll-and-whip the edge of the fabric, then work the crocheting.

Round 1. Work 311 sc evenly around edge of the fabric; sl st into 1st sc.

Rnd 2. (3 ch, sk, 2 dc, 1 sc into next sc.) Rept to end of rnd, sl st into the base of 1st 3-ch lp.

Rnd 3. Sl st into the center of the 1st 3-ch lp; 3 ch (count as 1 dc) 1 dc into next lp; *3 ch y.o.h, and insert into same 3-ch lp; draw yarn through 2 lps leaving 2 lps on hook; y.o.h and insert into next 3-ch lp, pull through 2 lps then 3 lps*. Rept to end of rnd; 3 ch; sl st into 3rd chn.

Crocheted Milk Jug Cover.

Rnd 4. Work a sl st into next dc and into center of the 3-ch lp; *5 ch, 1 dc into next 3-ch lp*. Rept to end of rnd; sl st into 1st sc.

Rnd 5. Sl st into center of 5 ch lp; 5 dc into next dc; 1 dc into next 5 ch lp; *(5 dc into next dc) twice (3 fans made); 1 dc into next 5-ch lp; 5 dc,1 dc into next lp; 5 ch, 1 dc into next lp (two 5-ch lps made)*. Rept from * to * to end of rnd; sl st into 1st dc.

Rnd 6. Sl st into the 3rd dc of the 1st fan; 3 ch (count as 1 dc), 5 ch, sk 1 dc of next fan; 1 dc into next dc; 2 dc into next dc; 1 dc into next dc (square made). *5 ch, 1 dc into 3rd dc of next fan; 5 ch, y.o.h and insert into next 5-ch lp; draw through 2 lps leaving 2 lps on hook; y.o.h and insert into next 5-ch lp.; draw through 2 lps then 3 lps (upside down V made); 5 ch, 1 dc into 3rd dc of next fan; 5 ch, sk 1st dc of next fan; 1 dc into the 2nd dc; 2 dc into next dc; 1 dc into next dc*. Rept from * to * to end of rnd; sl st into 3rd ch.

Rnd 7. Sl st into next 5 ch and next 4 dc; 3 ch (count as 1 dc), 3 dc into next lp; *5 ch, 1 dc into next 2 lps; 5 ch, 3 dc into next lp; 1 dc into last dc of sq; 3 dc into next lp*. Repeat from * to * to end of rnd; 19 ch, sl st into 3rd chain.

Rnd 8. Sl st into next 3 dc; *3 ch (count as 1 dc); 3 dc into next 5-ch lp; *5 ch, 1 dc into next lp; 5 ch 3 dc into next lp; 1 dc into 1st dc of sq; 5 ch, 1 dc into center of 10-ch lp; 5 ch, 1 dc into last dc of next sq; 3 dc into next lp*. Rept from * to * to end of rnd; sl st into 3rd chain.

Rnd 9. Sl st into next 3 dc; 3 ch (count as 1 dc), 3 dc into next 5-ch lp; *5 ch, 3 dc into next 5-ch lp, 1 dc into 1st dc of sq; 5 ch, 1 dc into next lp; 1 dc into next dc; 1 dc into next 5-ch lp; 5 ch, 1 dc into last dc of sq; 3 dc into next lp*. Rept from * to * to end of rnd; sl st into 3rd ch.

Rnd 10. Sl st into next 3 dc; 3 ch (count as 1 dc), 7 dc into 5 ch lp; 1 dc into 1 dc of sq; *9 dc, 1 dc into next 5 ch lp; 1 dc into next 3 dc; 1 dc into next 5 ch lp; 1 dc into last dc of sq*. Rept from * to * to end of rnd, sl st into 3rd ch.

Rnd 11. 3 ch (count as 1 dc); *3 dc into next 3 dc; 5 ch, sk 1 dc; 1 dc into next 4 dc; 3 dc into 9-ch lp; 9 ch, sk 1 dc; 1 dc into next 3 dc; 9 ch, 3 dc into 9-ch lp; 1 dc into next dc.* Rept from * to * to the last spider; sk 1 dc, 1 dc into next 3 dc; 9 ch; 3 dc into 9-ch lp; sl st into 3rd ch.

Rnd 12. 3 ch (count as 1 dc); *7 ch, 1 dc into next 5 ch lp; 7 ch, sk 3 dc, 1 dc into next 4 dc; 3 dc into next 9-ch lp; 9 ch, sk 1 dc; 1 dc into next dc; 9 ch, sk 1 dc, 3 dc into next 9-ch lp; 4 dc into next dc*. Rept * to * to last spider; 9 ch, sk 1 dc, 1 dc into next dc; 9 ch, 3 dc in next 9 ch lp; sl st into 3 ch.

Rnd 13. 3 ch (count as 1 dc); *7 ch, sk 3 ch; 1 dc, 2 ch, 1 dc into next ch; 5 ch, sk 3 ch, 1 dc, 2 ch, 1 dc into next ch; 7 ch, sk 3 dc, 4 dc into next 4 dc; 3 dc into next 9-ch lp; 2 ch, 3 dc into next 9-ch lp; 1 dc into next 4 ch*. Rept from * to * to end of rnd; sl st into 3rd ch.

Rnd 14. 3 ch (count as 1 dc); *5 ch; 1 dc, 2 ch, 1 dc into the center of 7-ch lp; 5 ch; 1 dc, 5 ch, 1 dc into center of 2nd 7-ch lp; 5 ch, 1 dc, 2 ch, 1 dc into center of 3rd 7-ch lp; 5 ch, sk 3 dc; 1 dc into next 4 dc; 2 dc into 2-ch lp; 4 dc into next 4 dc*. Rept from * to * to end of rnd; sl st into 3 ch. Finish off thread.

Rnd 15. Join thread into 2nd of the 10 dc (on top of spider); 3 ch (count as 1 dc); 7 dc into next 7 dc; *7 ch, 1 dc into 2-ch lp; 7 ch, 4 dc, 5-ch; 4 dc into next 5-ch lp; 7 ch, 1 dc into next 8 dc*. Rept from * to * to end of rnd; sl st into 3rd ch.

Rnd 16. Sl st into next dc; 3 ch (count as 1 dc); 1 dc into next 5 dc; *7 ch, 1 dc into next 7-ch loop; 7 ch (y.o.h and insert into 1st dc; draw through 2 lps leaving 2 lps on hook) rept twice; y.o.h insert into 4th dc; draw yarn through all 5 lps (dle acorn made); 3 dc, 4 dc, 5 ch, 4 dc into next 5-ch lp; 3 ch, 1 dle acorn into next 4 dc; 7 ch, 1 dc into next 7-ch lp; 7 ch; sk 1 dc; 1 dc into next 6dc*. Rept from * to * to end of rnd; sl st into 3rd ch.

Rnd 17. Sl st into next dc; 3 ch (count as 1 dc), 1 dc into next dc; 3 ch, sl st into 1st ch,1 ch (picot made); 1 dc into next 2 dc; *7 ch; sk 1 dc and the 7-ch lp; 1 dc into next 7-ch lp; 7 ch, sk 1 dle acorn and 3-ch lp; 1 dle acorn into next 4 dc, 3 ch into next lp; (y.o.h twice, draw yarn through 2 lps twice, leaving 2 lps on hook) 3 times; y.o.h twice, draw yarn through 2 lps then through all 5 remaining lps (tr acorn made); 5 ch, 1 tr acorn into same lp as previous tr acorn; 3 ch, 1 dle acorn into next 4 dc; 7 ch, sk 7-ch lp; 1 dc into next 7-ch lp; 7 ch, sk 1 dc; 1 dc into next 2 dc; 1 picot; 1 dc into next 2 dc*. Rept from * to * to end of rnd; sl st into 3rd ch.

Finishing

Secure the yarn and finish off the thread. Sew the beads onto the ends of the peaks.

Victorian Flowerpot

kitchen knife
Oasis block
terracotta or brass pot
quick-drying craft glue
Spanish moss
assorted dried and silk flowers; i.e. dried rosebuds,
lavender, larkspur, hydrangea, wheat, dried grass
ruler
florist's cutters
decorative ribbon
scissors

Use the kitchen knife to trim the Oasis florist's foam block to fit tightly in the pot.

Lavender and dried rosebuds Victorian Flowerpot.

You may need to add a few dots of glue to secure the Oasis. Place a thin layer of Spanish moss over the Oasis. This will be held in place by the stems of the dried flowers.

Before cutting the stems of the flowers, decide on the design for your Victorian Flowerpot. If your pot is round, then you might arrange the flowers in a circular fashion, starting from the center and working out.

The flowers can be graded in height, shorter as you reach the outside of the pot, or even in height overall.

To decide on the height of the flowers use the following examples: a 5 in. (13 cm) pot will need flowers approximately 12½ in. (32 cm) in length (including the heads), and a 3 in. (8 cm) pot will need flowers approximately 8 in. (20 cm) in length. Cut all the flower stems before beginning to arrange them in the pot.

Starting from the center of the pot and working your way out, push in each stem until the flower heads are exactly the same height; or grade the height of each different type of flower alternately for a different effect. Arrange the flowers in an orderly fashion with the heads just touching. Continue until the pot is completely filled. Cut a piece of ribbon to wrap firmly around the stems of the dried flowers.

Glue the ribbon around the flowers, halfway between the top of the pot and the top of the flowers. Cut two 3 in. (8 cm) lengths of ribbon (for tails) and glue these onto the ribbon band at a 45-degree angle.

Cut a 10 in. (25 cm) length of the ribbon, fold it in half lengthwise to find the center and mark it. Place the ribbon right side down on your working surface; bring the ends to the center, overlapping them by ⅜ in. (10 mm) to form a bow. Glue to hold. Cut a 2½ in. (6 cm) length of ribbon, wrap it around the center join of the bow and glue to hold. Glue the bow over the top of the ribbon streamers.

As an option, glue the same ribbon around the top edge of the pot.

Lavender Bottles

(enough for one Lavender Bottle)
about 13 lavender stalks (always use an odd
number of stalks)
1⅔ yd (1.5 m) of ³/₁₆ in. (5 mm) ribbon
rubber band

Pick the lavender just before the flowers open; leave stems approximately 8 in. (20 cm) long.

Neatly bunch the heads and tie the piece of ribbon just below the flowers, to hold the stalks together (diagram 1). Use the full length of ribbon, leaving it to trail at one end.

Tip the lavender stems upside down and gently fold them, one at a time, down over the flower heads, to form a kind of cage (diagram 2).

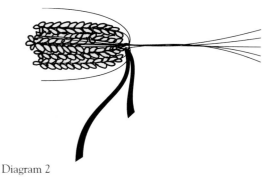

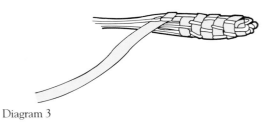

Diagram 2

Diagram 3

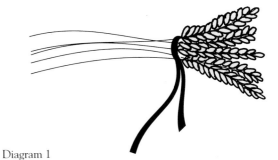

Diagram 1

Then weave the length of the ribbon over and under the stems to form a "basket" with the flower heads inside (diagram 3). Knot the ribbon at the base of the woven basket and finish with a bow.

Place the rubber band around the base of the stems to stop them from spreading out as they dry.

Lavender Bottles are simple and quick to make and are perfect for freshening linen.

Potpourri Lace Fan

pencil, ruler, scissors
thick cardboard (pasteboard)
spray adhesive
batting (wadding)
20 x 14 in. (50 x 35 cm) lace fabric
potpourri
quick-drying craft glue
78 in. (2 m) of ⅛ in. (3 mm) wide ribbon
20 in. (50 cm) of 1⅛ in. (3 cm) wide gathered lace
10 in. (25 cm) of 4 in. (10 cm) wide scalloped lace
20 in. (50 cm) insertion lace ribbon
20 x 14 in. (50 x 35 cm) fabric
small dried roses and greenery

Enlarge the scaled pattern as instructed on page 141 and transfer to the cardboard. Cut out two cardboard pieces. Lightly spray-glue one piece to the batting (wadding) and leave to dry. Trim the batting (wadding) neatly around the edges of the cardboard.

Cut out the lace fabric to cover this piece, allowing an extra 1⅛ in. (3 cm) around the edges, and set aside. Spread a thin, even layer of potpourri over the batting (wadding). Lay the fabric (right side up) over the potpourri and carefully turn the fan piece over to the cardboard side, making sure not to spill any of the potpourri.

Apply quick-drying glue around the edges of the pasteboard and, as neatly as possible, bring the lace fabric "hem" over and stick it down.

Decorate the front of the fan with strips of the ⅛ in. (3 mm) ribbon, using the dotted lines on the pattern as a guide.

Glue the gathered lace around the top of the fan on the cardboard side (diagram 1).

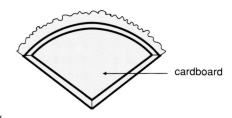

cardboard

Diagram 1

Glue the scalloped lace across the base of the front of the fan, turning the ends over and gluing them to the back.

Cut the non-lace fabric to cover the other cardboard piece plus 1⅛ in. (3 cm) all around. Using the spray glue, attach the wrong side of the fabric to the cardboard. Turn the fan piece over to the cardboard side, apply quick-drying glue around the edges, then bring the fabric over to adhere.

Using the tip of the scissors, make two small holes on the fabric side in the hole positions shown on the pattern. Use the remaining 20 in. (50 cm) of the ⅛ in. (3 mm) ribbon to thread through the holes and knot at the back (cardboard side). Apply glue to the back of both pieces and press together securely.

Fold the insertion lace ribbon into a bow and glue to the base of the fan at the front.

Glue on the small dried roses and the greenery. Tie the remaining ribbon into a bow and glue it under the flowers.

Potpourri Lace Fan.

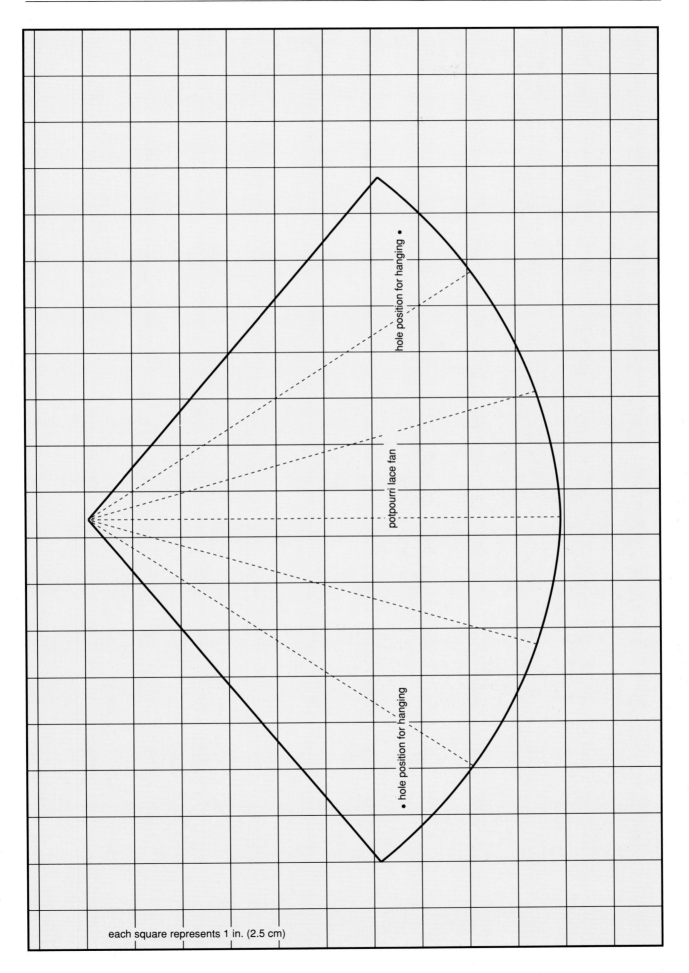

hole position for hanging •

potpourri lace fan

• hole position for hanging

each square represents 1 in. (2.5 cm)

CHAPTER 5

Victorian Christmas

By the 1880s Christmas was again being celebrated throughout the Christian world, after centuries of neglect following the Reformation. In the months leading up to Christmas, Victorians spent many hours making handmade gifts and decorations in preparation for the festive period. Elaborate Christmas cards were circulated, and lavishly trimmed *Tannenbaums* (Christmas trees), laden with wrapped gifts, were displayed in most homes. Food was prepared in great abundance, and inviting odors permeated the house. Candles were lit to complete the festive atmosphere. A Victorian Christmas was a particularly lavish affair, and many of its traditions remain to the present day.

Above: A section of Crazy Patchwork taken from the Christmas Tree Skirt.
Opposite: A typical Victorian Christmas setting.

Crazy Patchwork Christmas Tree Skirt

10 in. (25 cm) of 6 to 8 Christmasy fabrics (these can include velvet, satin, cotton)
4 ft (1.2 m) plain fabric for the lining
4 ft (1.2 m) muslin for the foundation of the crazy patchwork
7¾ yd (7 m) beading with gathered lace edges and a length of ribbon to thread through it
20 in. (50 cm) of bias binding
assorted ribbons, lace, embroidery floss, beads, trinkets, buttons, and other embellishments
tracing (graphite) paper
pencil, scissors, pins, iron

Embroidery stitches used:

herringbone stitch
chevron stitch
chain stitch
feather stitch

Enlarge the scaled pattern as instructed on page 4 and transfer the notches. A ¼ in. (6 mm) seam allowance is included on the outer edge only. Cut the four sections for each panel from the foundation muslin.

Cover each section with crazy patchwork following the instructions for piecing on page 147. Then cover the seams in the patchwork with old-fashioned embroidery stitches such as herringbone stitch, chevron stitch, feather stitch, and chain stitch, or with lace and beads. (Antique buttons and other small treasures are also excellent embellishments.)

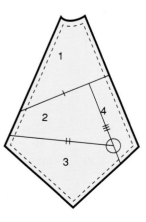

Diagram 1

Instructions for the stitches are included in the Stitch Glossary on pages 158–164. Butt each of the four sections together to make a panel, by first stitching 2 to 3, then stitch on 4, and then 1 (see diagram 1).

Stitch the lace-edged beading over the seams joining sections 2 and 3, then the seam of 2, 3, and 4, making sure the lace hides the join marked on diagram 1 with O. Finally, stitch the beading over the seam

Crazy Patchwork was popular during the Victorian era, and is beautifully shown in this tree skirt and stocking.

joining 2, 3, and 4 to 1. Thread ribbon through each piece of the beading before adding the next panel. When you have completed eight panels as described, join all eight together with a ¼ in. (6 mm) seam, leaving one seam open so the skirt can wrap around the tree.

Cut eight panels from the lining fabric and stitch the seams in the same manner.

With the right sides together, carefully stitch the outside edges of the tree skirt and the lining together, matching points and corners, leaving the top open to turn. Clip the inner corners and trim excess fabric from the outer corners. Turn to the right side and press carefully. Bind the curved top edge with the bias binding. Stitch on the ribbon ties to keep in position around the tree.

Christmas Stocking

6 in. (15 cm) of 6 to 8 Christmasy fabrics
(these can include velvet, satin, cotton)
20 in. (50 cm) plain fabric for lining
20 in. (50 cm) muslin for foundation of the crazy
patchwork
16 in. (40 cm) bias binding
1 yd 16 in. (130 cm) beading with gathered lace edges
to cover the joins on the front and back of the stocking
pins
pencil
tracing (graphite) paper
scissors
assorted ribbons, lace, embroidery threads, beads,
trinkets, and other embellishments
iron

Embroidery stitches used:
herringbone stitch
chevron stitch
feather stitch
chain stitch

Enlarge the scaled pattern as instructed on page 4 and trace the pattern pieces, including all the notches. A ¼ in. (6 mm) seam allowance is included on the outside edges only. Using the muslin foundation, cut the three sections for the front and three for the back.

Work each piece with crazy patchwork individually, following the instructions on page 147 for piecing crazy patchwork. Embellish the seams in the patchwork with old-fashioned embroidery stitches such as herringbone stitch, chevron stitch, feather stitch, and the lace and beads. Antique buttons and other small treasures are also excellent embellishments. Instructions for the embroidery stitches are in the Stitch Glossary on pages 158–164.

When the six pieces are embellished to your satisfaction, butt the notched edges of these three front pieces together and zigzag on the sewing machine. Repeat the process for the three back pieces. Cover the two seams on the front and the two on the back with the lace beading.

With the right sides together, stitch the stocking front to the back with a ¼ in. (6 mm) seam. Clip the curves and turn to the right side. Press carefully.

Cut out a front and a back stocking from the lining fabric. Stitch them together with a ¼ in. (6 mm) seam. Do not turn. Push lining down into the stocking and pin in place. Bind the top edge with the bias binding, turning the ends down into the inside of the stocking, and slip stitching in place. Add lace to the top if desired and stitch on a ribbon loop to hang it up by. Decorate with ribbon bows and bells to complete.

Crazy Patchwork is known for its intricate embroidery and elaborate embellishments.

Crazy Patchwork Piecing

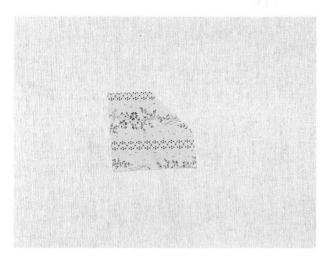

Stage 1

Cut the center shape with five sides, approximately 2 x 2 in. (5 x 5 cm) with one corner cut off.

Stage 2

Cut the first strip large enough to cover the center shape. Lay right sides together, then stitch with ¼ in. (6 mm) seam, turn over and press. Trim level with side 2.

Stage 3

Cut the second strip and lay it along side 2 of the central piece. Be sure that the strip extends beyond the first one. Sew from the edge of that previous piece to the edge of this second piece. Trim. Turn over and press.

Continue clockwise around the center piece until all five sides are covered.

Stage 4

Note: The piece that covers side 5 also covers the ends of the pieces along sides 4 and 1.

Stage 5

Continue adding pieces in a clockwise direction until the foundation muslin is completely covered. Trim the outside edges even with the foundation.

Stage 6

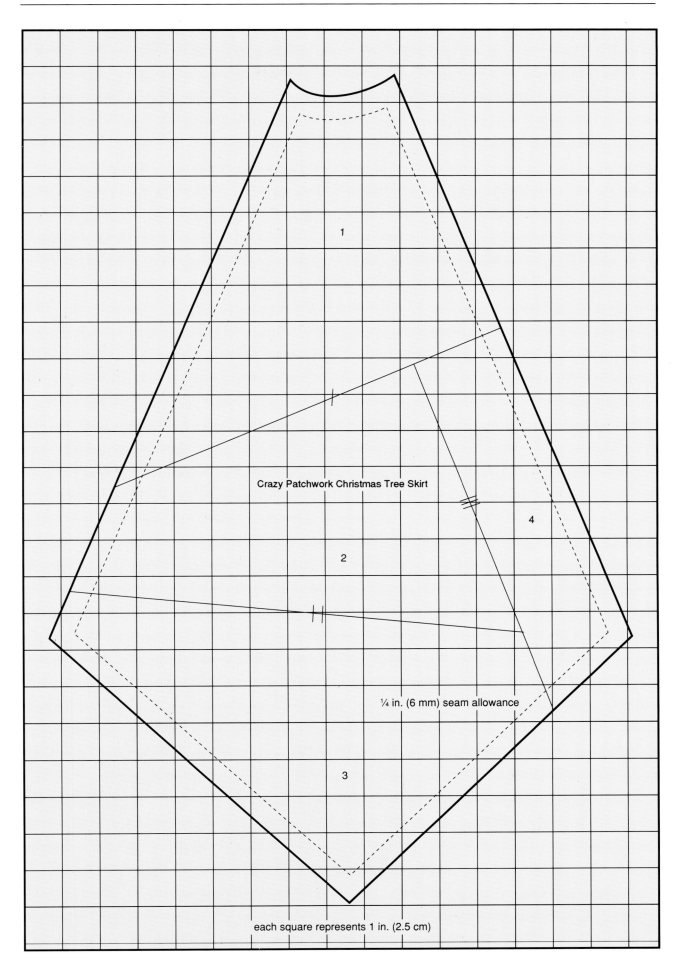

1

Crazy Patchwork Christmas Tree Skirt

4

2

¼ in. (6 mm) seam allowance

3

each square represents 1 in. (2.5 cm)

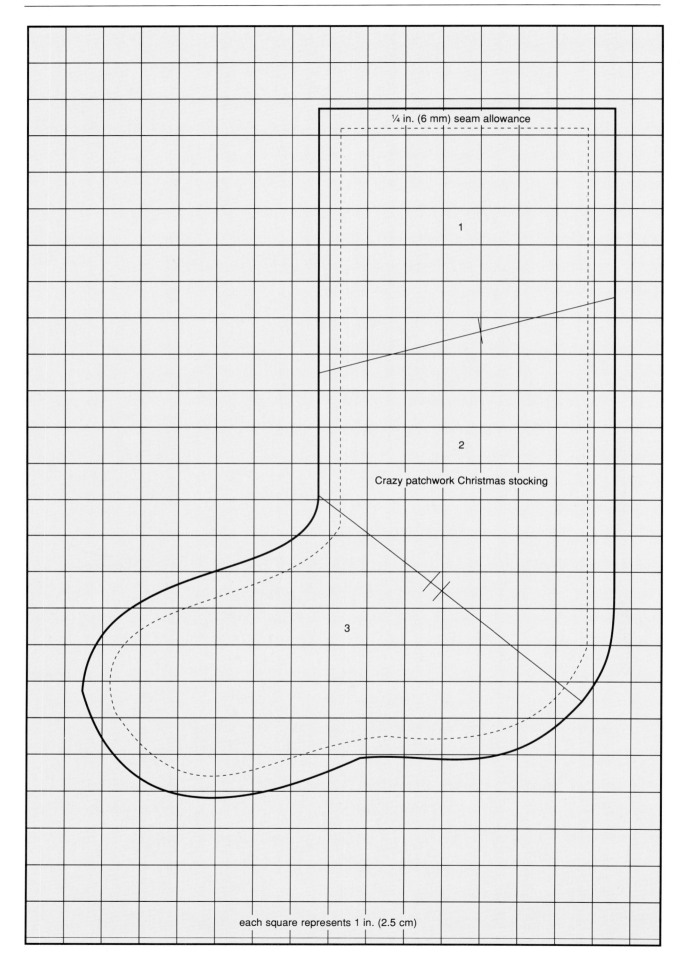

¼ in. (6 mm) seam allowance

1

2

Crazy patchwork Christmas stocking

3

each square represents 1 in. (2.5 cm)

Napkin Rings

To make 4 napkin rings:
1 cardboard roll at least 6 in. (15 cm) long
Christmasy fabric
26 in. (66 cm) of ⅝ in. (16 mm) wide gold ribbon
polyester batting (wadding)
narrow gathered lace
gold silk flowers
dark red berries, green leaves
sharp knife
ruler, pencil
scissors
quick-drying craft glue

Cut the cardboard roll into four rings 1½ in. (4 cm) wide, using the sharp knife. Measure and cut strips of batting (wadding) to cover the outside of the rings and glue on. Measure and cut the fabric ⅜ in. (10 mm) larger than the rings and glue on, overlapping the fabric where it meets and turning the fabric under the inside edge of the ring. Glue the narrow gathered lace to the inside edge of the ring so that the ruffles stick out. Cut a strip of gold ribbon long enough to wrap around the ring and overlap by ⅜ in. (10 mm) and glue on. Arrange and glue on the leaves, berries, and silk flowers to cover the overlap of the gold ribbon.

Christmas Centerpiece

thick cardboard, compass, pencil
polyester batting (wadding)
assorted ribbons and lace, green garland
gold pine cones, imitation oak leaves, berries
one 5 in. (12.5 cm) polystyrene ball
candle
Christmasy fabric, pearl string
scissors, quick-drying craft glue
sharp knife, florist's wire

Draw a 12 in. (30.5 cm) diameter circle on the thick cardboard, using the compass, and cut out. Cut a piece of batting (wadding) the same size and glue it onto the cardboard circle.

Cut one piece of Christmas fabric 1 in. (2.5 cm) larger than the circle. Covering the batting (wadding), attach the fabric to the cardboard with glue. Cut another piece of the fabric the exact size of the covered cardboard and glue to the underside. Glue the lace onto the edge of the underside.

Cut the foam ball in half and glue one half onto the center of the batting (wadding) covered side of the circle. Cut the green garland into small pieces and glue onto the ball until it is completely covered. Loop the assorted ribbons and arrange on the ball, glue in place. Glue a row of wide lace around the edge of the ball. Arrange the oak leaves and the pearl loops alternately, just under the edge of the lace, and glue in place (diagram 1). Arrange the pine cones, berries, and assorted ribbon and lace loops over the ball and glue or wire in place. Push a candle carefully into the center of the ball and glue into position.

Diagram 1

Following pages: From front, Napkin Rings, Christmas Crackers, Christmas Centerpiece and Small Christmas Tree.

Small Christmas Tree

large cone of Oasis rigid foam
dried hydrangeas sprayed gold
3¼ yd (3 m) of ⅛ in. (3 mm) wide dark red ribbon
3¼ yd (3 m) of ⅛ in. (3 mm) wide green ribbon
3¼ yd (3 m) of narrow gold ribbon
scissors, wire cutters, florist's wire
2 circles of thick cardboard 6 in. (15 cm) in diameter
assorted Christmas decorations—holly, berries,
baubles, pine cones, acorns
Christmas-print fabric:
1 piece 7 x 19¾ in. (18 x 50 cm)
2 pieces 8 in. square (20 x 20 cm)
19¾ in. (50 cm) of narrow gold braid
quick-drying craft glue, needle and thread

Split up the gold-sprayed hydrangeas into small pieces. Glue the petals evenly over the Oasis cone, except for the base. All the Christmasy decorations have to be wired separately before being pushed into the cone, or alternatively they can be glued on. When placing the decorations on the cone, always remember to range from the largest at the bottom to the smallest at the top. It is easier to wire the pieces first and then decorate the tree using one type of decoration at a time, thus making sure all the items are evenly spaced.

Make an assortment of small wired ribbon loops, using the red, green, and gold ribbon, to add color to the tree and to fill any remaining spaces.

Ruffle for the Base of "Tree"

Fold the large oblong piece of fabric in half lengthwise and press. Sew or glue the narrow gold braid onto the fabric ⅜ in. (10 mm) in from the folded edge. Gather up the fabric to fit around the base of the Oasis cone, then secure and glue onto the base around the edge.

Smear glue over one side of each of the cardboard circles and adhere to the pre-cut 8 in. square (20 x 20 cm) pieces of fabric.

Trim the fabric back to ¾ in. (20 mm) all around and snip into the circle to allow the fabric to turn over smoothly. Apply glue around the edge of the cardboard on the back, turn the fabric to the back and hold firmly until the glue is dry. Run a line of glue around the edge of the wrong side of one of the covered circles. Place both wrong sides together. Allow to dry and then glue to the base of the cone.

Christmas Crackers

To make one cracker only:
6 x 8 in. (15 x 20 cm) piece of firm white paper
5½ in. (14 cm) long cardboard roll
2 small gold seals, 2 gold berries, 1 gold paper doily
6 x 8 in. (15 x 20 cm) piece of white crepe paper
quick-drying craft glue, scissors
friction strip, if available in your area
6¼ in. (16 cm) of 9⅞ in. (25 cm) wide dark
red ribbon
12½ in. (32 cm) of ¼ in. (6 mm) wide gold ribbon
25¼ in. (64 cm) of ⅛ in. (3 mm) wide green ribbon
27½ in. (70 cm) of ⅛ in. (3 mm) wide
dark red ribbon, scrap of gold tinsel

Glue the white crepe paper and the firm white paper together by squeezing a thin line of glue around one edge. Insert the friction strip as per the manufacturer's instructions. If this strip, which produces the cracking sound, is not available, insert a decorative ribbon with an inexpensive party favor tied to it.

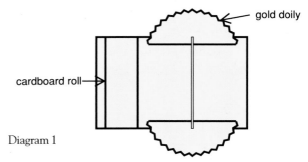

Diagram 1

Lay the firm white paper covered with crepe paper onto a flat surface. Fold and cut the doily in half and glue the two pieces on either edge (see diagram 1).

Place the cardboard roll at the edge of the firm paper (see diagram 1) and roll the paper around the roll, glue the final edge down. Cut the ⅛ in. (3 mm) dark red ribbon into two 9⅞ in. (25 cm) lengths and an 8 in. (20 cm) length. Tie the two longer pieces around the two ends of the crackers, pinching the doily in and tying bows. Wrap the wider dark red ribbon around the center of the cracker, glue in place. Wrap the thin gold ribbon around each end with the green ribbon either side of it and glue at the back. Fasten the gold seals on the top. Decorate the wide dark red ribbon with the tinsel, gold berries, and red ribbon loops.

Christmas crackers can be used as decorations on the table or the tree and are pulled apart by two people firmly grasping each of the ends and tugging. The "winner" is the one who receives the end with the treat.

Patchwork Tree Decorations

assorted polystyrene shapes (balls, bells)
selection of Christmasy fabrics (at least four)
gold braids, gold buttons, beads, sequins, "pearls"
quick-drying craft glue
craft knife, scissors, pins
small screwdriver or metal nail file

Choose a combination of fabrics that complement each other, such as small prints, narrow stripes, and large prints, so that an interesting pattern is obtained on your decorations.

Before cutting into the polystyrene shape, decide on a pattern. The patterns can be in true patchwork form, either symmetrical or in a "crazy" fashion. Using the craft knife to the full length of the blade, cut the pattern into the shape. Complete all the pattern lines before continuing. Cut the fabric pieces 1 in. (2.5 cm) larger than the shapes. With a small screwdriver or nail file, carefully push the fabric into the sliced foam until one section is completely covered. Repeat until all the pattern sections are covered. Decorate along the edges where the fabric meets with pearls, lace and braids.

Glue sequins, beads, and small gold buttons on the polystyrene shapes. Loop pearls or gold ribbon at the top and bottom, using pins dipped in glue to hold.

Patchwork Tree Decorations.

Smocked Christmas Ball

44¼ x 5½ in. (112 x 14 cm) ecru cotton batiste
ecru floss, gold metallic floss = C1
dark red stranded embroidery floss = C2
27½ in. (70 cm) of ⅛ in. (3 mm) double-sided
satin ribbon—cream
19¾ in. (50 cm) of ⅛ in. (3 mm) double-sided
satin ribbon—dark red
two pieces of 8 in. (20 cm) ecru lace edging
⅜ in. (10 mm) wide
gold seed beads, dark red seed beads, gold sequins
3 in. (7.5 cm) polystyrene ball
No. 7 crewel embroidery needle
quick-drying craft glue, pins

Pleat up 11 rows. Use a double thread the same color as the fabric on the top and bottom rows. Pull threads back to allow a ³⁄₁₆ in. (5 mm) seam. Tie off in pairs to measure 7½ in. (19 cm). Count the pleats and mark the center on the right side. Smock the ball according to the instructions, using two strands of the embroidery floss. The beads are added while smocking; a second stitch will hold the beads securely.

The Smocking Pattern

Following the graph, begin to smock the design, working from the center to ensure continuity.
Row 1. C1 (gold) smock outline stitch.
Row 9. C1 smock stem stitch.
Row 1½. C2 (dark red) smock ½ space waves (chevrons).
Row 8½. C2 as above.
Row 1½–2½. Smock ½ space waves as on graph. Gold beads are added to alternate up-cables at row 1½ level.
Row 8½–7½. Same ½ space wave pattern. Beads are added to alternate down-cables at row 8½ level.
Row 5. C1 smock 4-step full space trellis, 4 cables, 3-step full space trellis combination. Contrast bead is added to up-cable at row 3 level.
Row 4¾. C1 smock as above.
Row 4½. C2 smock as above.
Row 4½. C2 smock as above. Gold bead is added to up-cable at 2¼ row level.

Rows 5–7¾. Smock as above forming a mirror image. Fill in the center with trellis, working diagonally across from point to point.

Finishing

When the smocking has been completed, leave the top and bottom double threads in the fabric and remove all the other gathering threads. Fold, and with the right sides together match the design and stitch down the seam allowance, to form a cylinder. Turn right side out. Insert the ball into the smocked cylinder and secure the smocking to the ball with straight pins pushed all the way in. Gather the top and the bottom threads in to fit the ball and tie off securely. Carefully trim off the excess fabric and fold the fabric toward the center. Stitch in place holding the folds flat to the ball.

Decorate the top of the ball with ribbon loops for hanging and the bottom with lace, sequins and beads. Gather the lace edging to form a circle and secure with glue. Secure the ribbon loops with pins dipped in glue and pushed into the ball. Secure the sequins by placing a matching sequin and bead on a pin and pushing into the ball in a tight circle for approximately three rows.

The Smocked Christmas Ball.

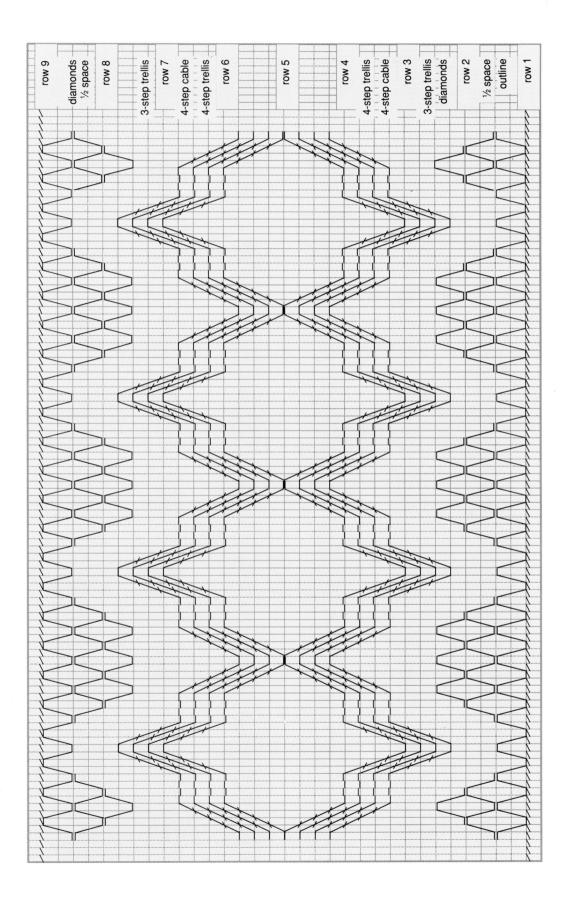

row 9

diamonds
½ space

row 8

3-step trellis

row 7

4-step cable

4-step trellis

row 6

row 5

row 4

4-step trellis

4-step cable

row 3

3-step trellis
diamonds

row 2

½ space
outline

row 1

Stitch Glossary

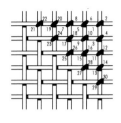

Basketweave Stitch

Worked in diagonal rows up and down. This stitch obtains its name from the appearance on the wrong side of the work, but is identical in appearance to continental stitch on the right side of the work. Basketweave stitch does not distort the canvas as much as continental stitch, although it does use more thread.

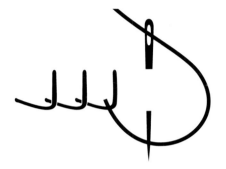

Blanket Stitch — *see* Buttonhole Stitch

Blanket stitch is the same as buttonhole stitch except that the upright stitches are placed much farther apart.

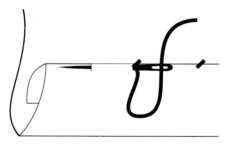

Blind Stitch

Turn either one or both raw edges of the fabric under the desired amount, and finger press. Run the needle ¼ in. (6 mm) inside the fabric fold and bring the needle and thread out again. Pick up one or two threads on the single layer of the fabric, or on the other folded edge, and pull the thread through firmly. Continue picking up one or two threads on one side after the other.

Buttonhole Stitch

Buttonhole stitch is a simple, looped line stitch and has a variety of applications, both practical and decorative. It is frequently used for finishing raw edges as well as for buttonholes. Work buttonhole stitch from left to right, pulling the needle through the fabric and over the working thread; this action forms a row of vertical straight stitches joined together by a looped edge at the bottom. The stitch is equally successful worked in straight lines or following curves, and the size of the vertical stitches can be graduated to give a wavy line or a saw-toothed edge at the top of the row. The stitches are placed closely together, so that no ground fabric shows between them; if they are widely spaced, the stitch is known as blanket stitch.

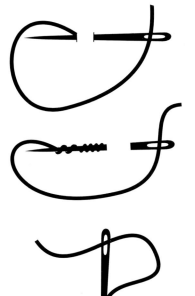

Bullion Stitch (or Knot)

A bullion stitch is an isolated stitch that is actually a long, coiled knot. A bullion knot is easier to do if it is worked on fabric stretched tight in an embroidery hoop. The distance between the point where the needle is inserted and the place where the point emerges determines the length of the knot, this way: insert the needle point and then bring the point up at the distance you want the knot to cover; wrap the thread around the exposed point of the needle six or seven times, then pull the needle all the way out carefully through the wraps, which you hold back firmly with the left thumb (if you are right-handed). Gently pull the working thread in the opposite direction to tighten the wraps and, holding the wraps down on the fabric, insert the needle in exactly the same place you inserted it before and pull it back to the underside of the cloth.

Chain Stitch

Chain stitch is simple to work and the stitches should be kept even and the same size. Take the thread under the needle and do not pull right through, this makes the oval shape of the stitch.

Chevron Stitch

Chevron stitch is worked from left to right between two parallel lines, in a way similar to herringbone stitch. It is composed of diagonal stitches set at an angle, with a shorter horizontal stitch worked where these stitches meet. To keep the width of the stitches even guidelines can be marked on the fabric.

Colonial Knot

A colonial knot is firmer than a French knot and sits up well on the top of the fabric.

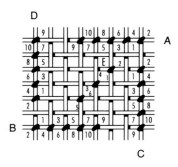

Continental Stitch

Use continental/tent stitch for outlining the design area and basketweave stitch for filling in and for background areas. Continental stitch can be worked in five directions, as shown in the diagram and indicated by the letters alongside. The numbers indicate the order of stitching.

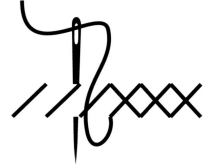

Cross Stitch

Cross stitch is made of a series of diagonal stitches, worked in both directions (crossed): work the bottom stitches across the row from left to right and then come back, working the top diagonal stitches from right to left. Always keep the top diagonal stitches lying in the same direction.

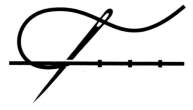

Couching Stitch

A thread or cord is laid down against the fabric and held in place by a second, lighter thread. Couching is worked from right to left, usually along a marked line. Hold the laid-down cord in place and guide with your left hand (if you are right-handed) and make a small straight stitch over the laid-down thread. When working around curves, place the straight stitches closer together so that the cord lies flat.

Double Feather Stitch

This is a variation of feather stitch that is worked in a zigzag pattern. Work two or more stitches to each side, traveling downward. Keep the thread under the needle, do not pull the thread tight but allow it to curve as shown.

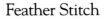

Feather Stitch

Feather stitch is worked downward by bringing the thread through at the top of the line to be covered and making a slanting loop stitch alternately to the left and to the right.

Fern Stitch

Fern stitch consists of groups of three straight stitches of equal length, worked at angles to each other and sharing the same base hole. The groups are arranged to form a line. It is essential that stitches be even in size and in spacing.

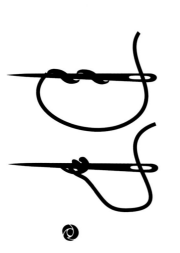

French Knot

French knots are best worked with the fabric stretched in an embroidery hoop or frame so as to leave both hands free for working. Bring the thread through the fabric and, if you are right-handed, hold it taut with the left hand while you twist the needle around it two or three times with the right hand. Then tighten the twists, turn the needle and push it back into the same place in the fabric. Still keeping the thread taut, and holding the twists in place with the left thumb, pull the needle through. The thread slides through the twists to make the knot.

Herringbone Stitch

Herringbone stitch is worked from left to right. You may want to draw a pair of guidelines to keep the stitches even.

Lazy Daisy (or Daisy Stitch)

Lazy daisy is formed in exactly the same way as chain stitch, but the loops are detached and each loop is anchored to the fabric by a small vertical stitch before the next loop is made. The size of the stitch is determined by the weight of embroidery thread used; any type of thread will work well.

Pistol Stitch

Pistol stitch is a Brazilian embroidery stitch and is worked differently every time, depending on the working instructions. The basic stitch is worked by coming up at a point, wrapping the needle and going down again at a given distance away from where the needle came up.

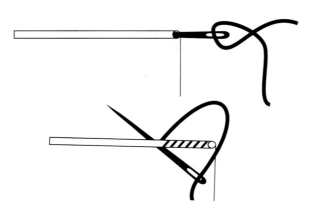

Rolled Hem (Roll-and-Whip)

This hand-sewing technique employing a roll-and-whip technique is used to finish off fabric edges and lace ends in heirloom sewing. Lay the needle horizontally along the top righthand corner of the fabric and roll the needle and the fabric down ¼ in. (6 mm). Remove the needle and slide the point under the roll and out the top, enclosing the roll but not going through the back of the fabric. Make the stitches ⅛ in. (3 mm) apart and keep the needle at a 45-degree angle.

Ribbon Stitch

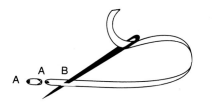

Ribbon stitch is used with silk ribbons. Bring the needle up at A, making sure the ribbon is flat and straight on the fabric. Hold the ribbon in place with your left thumb, and insert the needle through the ribbon at B. Take the needle through to the back of the background fabric and gently pull until the lip of the ribbon starts to curl back on itself and forms a point.

Satin Stitch

Satin stitch consists of straight stitches worked side by side. Care should be taken so that the stitches lie even and close to each other, completely covering the background fabric, and so that the outline is clean.

Stem Stitch

The stitch is worked with a forward-and-backward motion along the line; the stitches should be even and equal in size. The working thread must always be kept at the right of the needle; if it is at the left, the effect is slightly different, and the stitch is then known as an outline stitch.

Straight Stitch

Either a group or a single stitch that lies flat against the surface of the fabric, in various lengths.

Whip (Overcast) Stitch

Whip stitch is a hand-sewing technique used extensively in heirloom sewing. It is like a small overcasting stitch for attaching lace to lace, lace to fabric and entredeux to lace or fabric.

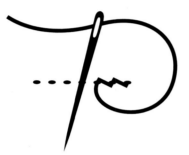

Whipped Running Stitch

Whipped (or threaded) running stitch makes a heavier line than an ordinary running stitch. First work a foundation of small, evenly spaced running stitches. Then whip a second thread through each of the stitches without picking up any of the background fabric.

Glossary

Acrylic paint Artist's color based on acrylic polymer resin and mixed with water.

Antiquing patina A type of lacquer used to emulate a surface beautified by age and use.

Batting Layers or sheets of cotton, wool or synthetic fibers, used for lining quilts or for stuffing. Wadding is similar, but comes as loose fibers rather than in sheets.

Beading needle A long needle with a fine eye.

Bias binding Binding for cloth, cut on the bias, used especially in hems.

Borax A white crystalline substance used as a cleansing agent.

Broderie beading A broderie lace with eyelet holes for threading ribbon through.

Bugle beads Small decorative beads that are sewn onto fabrics in clusters or designs.

Butting To join the edges of two things together.

Calico Small-printed cotton fabric (sprig muslin).

Candlewick thread Unbleached cotton thread used to represent the traditional craft of embroidering with the wick of a candle.

Carpenter's square (set square) Also known as a try square. A right-angled instrument used to test the squareness of work or for laying out right angles.

Chenille needle Like a tapestry needle but with a sharp point.

Clothes pin Old-fashioned solid wooden pegs now manufactured for craft in both round and flat profiles.

Couch To embroider with the thread laid flat on a surface and caught down at intervals.

Crackle medium A product used to emulate a network of fine cracks or weathered look.

Craftwood A type of wood sheeting made from compacted wood pulp.

Crewel embroidery needle The needle used for the majority of embroidery stitches.

Crosswise thread A thread that runs across the width of the fabric.

Damask Silk, linen or other fabric with figured pattern woven into it.

Decals Transfer pictures backed by paper and used to decorate surfaces such as china, glass, wood and metal.

DMC stranded embroidery floss A six-strand, divisible thread made of double mercerized, long staple, 100 percent cotton fibers available throughout the world.

DMC tapestry wool A non-divisible four-ply wool available throughout the world.

Enamel paint A type of paint which produces a bright, lustrous surface.

Entredeux A thin fabric strip used to join fabric and lace.

Fimo A brand name of a modeling material which when baked becomes hard like ceramic.

Florist's tape Used in floral arrangements, posies, etc. One type is Parafilm, a self-sealing tape that adheres when stretched.

French cotton lace A high quality 100 percent cotton-net-based lace.

French insertion lace A high quality 100 percent cotton lace with two straight edges.

French lace edging A high quality 100 percent cotton lace with one straight edge.

French seam A seam in which the edges of the cloth are sewn first on the right side, then on the wrong, so as to be completely enclosed.

Fusible webbing A fine webbed fabric that melts when exposed to heat and so will fuse to other materials such as fabric and wood.

Gathering stitches Long running stitches used to gather fabric.

Graphite paper Like carbon paper, a thin paper coated on one side with graphite, and used to transfer drawings, designs, etc. to other surfaces. Also called tracing paper.

Guipure lace A variety of laces, often heavy and made of silk or linen, with the pattern connected by heavy thread design rather than net.

Hank A definite length of thread or yarn.

Herringbone An embroidery stitch resembling cross stitch. Also, a pattern consisting of adjoining rows of parallel lines so arranged that any two rows have the form of a V.

Hot-melt glue gun An adhesive stick that, when subjected to heat through a trigger-action gun, melts and activates the adhesives.

Interfacing A fabric placed between outer material and facing to give body.

Lace beading Net-based lace with eyelet holes for threading ribbon through.

Lint-free cloth Clean cloth free of bits of thread or fluff known as lint.

Loading To take up paint on a brush for use in painting.

Loop turner An instrument used to turn any thin tube of fabric right side out.

Marlitt thread 100 percent viscose embroidery floss in a six-strand hank.

Masking tape An adhesive tape used for defining edges and protecting surfaces not to be painted.

Milliner's/straw needle Similar to a crewel embroidery needle but longer.

Miter The abutting surface or bevel on either of the pieces joined in a miter-joint.

Molded edges A decorative variety of contour or outline given to strips of woodwork, etc.

Muslin Off-white cotton fabric of plain weave.

Oasis A foam block used in floral arranging.

Organza A fine sheer fabric.

Pairing To weave cane over one stake, under the next, crossing the canes between the stakes.

Papier mâché A substance made of pulped paper mixed with glue and other materials. It is molded when moist to form shapes or layers of paper glued and pressed together.

Pellon A thin synthetic sheeting used for padding.

Pin tuck A fine tuck used especially as a decorative feature on a garment.

Plaster of Paris A white powdery material which swells when mixed with water and sets rapidly. Used for making casts, molds, etc.

Polyester batting (wadding) A synthetic sheeting used as a padding for quilting and a variety of craft work.

Potpourri A mixture of dried petals of roses or other flowers with spices and fixatives, kept in a jar for the fragrance.

Protractor A flat semicircular instrument that is graduated around the circular edge, used to measure or mark off angles.

PVA wood glue (Polyvinyl acetate) Used as an adhesive for materials with a porous surface such as wood, paper, leather, cloth, cardboard, where water resistance is not important.

Quick-drying craft glues Adhesives that contain solvents which evaporate as the glue dries, for quick adhesion.

Quilting thread A strong thread used for quilting.

Rouleau A cylindrical tube of fabric.

Roll-and-Whip A hand-sewing technique used for finished raw edges. See Stitch Glossary (page 162) for instructions.

Scoring The use of a stylus to form an indentation to facilitate folding.

Seam ripper A small sharp instrument used to remove incorrect stitching.

Seed beads Tiny decorative beads that are sewn in designs onto fabrics.

Selvage (selvedge) The edge of woven fabric finished to prevent fraying, often in a narrow tape effect.

Set square A flat piece of wood, plastic or the like in the shape of a right triangle, used in mechanical drawing.

Sewing tape A woven tape used in sewing to reinforce seams.

Slip stitch A small neat stitch used to close openings.

Smocking Embroidery stitches used to hold gathered cloth in a pattern of even folds.

Spanish moss A long greyish-green tufted plant that hangs from the branches of trees, found in Southern U.S.A. and the West Indies.

Spray adhesive An adhesive used for quick and easy bonding of large surfaces. Generally, spray adhesives give a temporary bond when sprayed onto one surface; however, if both surfaces are coated a permanent bond is achieved.

Stitch in the ditch To stitch in the seamline between two joined pieces or against the edge of entredeux.

Stucco technique Use of a special plaster mixture for cornices and moldings of rooms and for other decorations.

Stylus A pointed instrument used in drawing, in tracing and stenciling.

Swiss embroidered beading A fabric-based lace with an embroidered design and eyelet holes.

Swiss entredeux beading A fabric-based entredeux wide enough to thread ribbon through.

Swiss lace edging A fabric-based lace with an embroidered design and one straight edge.

Tacking stitch A temporary stitch used to hold layers in place for stitching.

Template A pattern or mold consisting of a thin plate of wood, metal or plastic used as a guide for transferring a design onto a work surface.

Toy filling A synthetic fiber used as stuffing.

Tracing paper A translucent paper used to copy designs by tracing. Also, in embroidery, used like carbon paper to transfer a pattern onto fabric (see Graphite paper).

Transfer paper A specially prepared paper used to transfer drawings and designs onto a work surface.

Tulle A thin silk or nylon net used in millinery and dressmaking.

Waling To weave over two stakes and under one.

Whip stitch A hand-sewing technique to attach lace to lace, lace to fabric, and entredeux to lace or fabric. See Stitch Glossary (page 164) for instructions.

White dressmaker's carbon A paper used to transfer patterns and designs onto dark fabric.

Wood sealer A liquid applied to the surface of wood prior to painting to form a seal and so prevent absorption.

Acknowledgments

For their assistance and expertise, the publishers wish to thank the following: Allison Kryvoviaza for the Miniature Victorian Doll's House • Jill Oxton for designing the Victorian Tapestry Doll and Maxine Henke for stitching it • Patricia Sutton for designing and stitching many of the embroidery and heirloom projects • Betty Kenear for the Rattan Rattle • Rae Archibald for her Crazy Patchwork Tree Skirt, Stocking, Embroidered Teddy Bear and Victorian Sewing Bag • Marilyn Salve for her many hours of craftwork • Raffial for the Raffia Hat • Eva Drummond and Elena Dickson for the crochet work • Diane Keller for the Brazilian Embroidery • Clair McBride for making the Hydrangea Swag • Jenny Bradford for her stitches used in My Diary • Leanne and José Milhano for the Hand-painted Lap Desk • Kerrie Akkermans and Oliver Greenwell for being models • XLN Fabrics for supplying the fabrics • Philippa Menzes for her cooperation with Ayers House.

AYERS HOUSE

Many thanks to the National Trust of South Australia for their assistance and generosity in offering the use of Ayers House as the photographic location for *Victorian Crafts*. Ayers House has been carefully restored to the original splendor of the Victorian era and is presented to the public by the National Trust.